HARVEST YOUR HAPPY

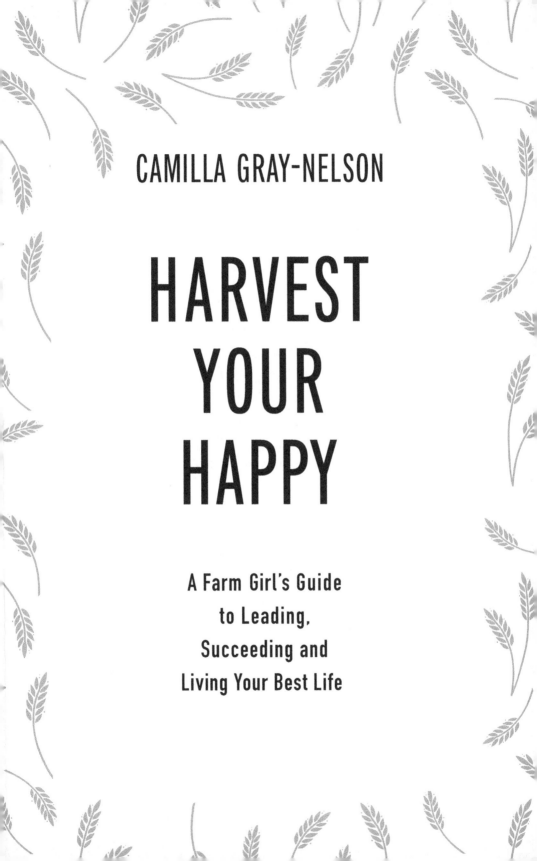

CAMILLA GRAY-NELSON

HARVEST YOUR HAPPY

A Farm Girl's Guide
to Leading,
Succeeding and
Living Your Best Life

DEDICATION

To my wonderful mother and father, who modeled for
me the precious elements of a contented and happy
life, with each other and with themselves.

To Monty Roberts, whose groundbreaking work with horses
brought Nature's miracle of quiet leadership to today's
human audience. His work inspired me to dig deeper into
Nature's lessons—from the barn to the boardroom.

and

To Bessy the Cow and Nellie the Dog, who finally taught
me how to succeed in business, guide young minds and
maintain a loving relationship

CONTENTS

PART TWO

Using Instincts and the Happiness Principles at Work, Parenting And Love

PREFACE

Modern Life is complicated, but relationships and finding happiness don't have to be. The simple path to Happy that I will share in this book doesn't require you to swipe left, have an ID, a password, or even an internet connection. It existed long before our lives got so wired and we all got so tired and the old ways of connecting with others were left in the dust of pre-pandemic life.

How do I know this? I found the secrets of relationship success, whether it's at home or at work, on *the farm!* Yes! Believe it or not, these secrets are what I learned from years of careful study and observation growing up on our family farm in Northern California and then working professionally for decades training animals and their people. With a lifetime of observation to call upon and a lifetime of experience to test my theories, I have a unique perspective on social success, unexpected tools to achieve it and the happiness that cannot thrive without it. I can't wait to share with you how to apply them to your present life.

I have come to realize that despite intelligence and socialization, we humans are still members of the Animal World! Hidden deep within us seem to lurk the very same instincts that drive and influence the behaviors of many other social mammals. Not only do our deepest instincts seem the same as those of other animals, but so can our processes of achieving and maintaining social harmony.

In *Harvest Your Happy,* I share my unique perspective and "field-tested" methods for growing healthy relationships, reducing friction and maximizing cooperation with anyone at any time in your life. My biggest hope is to share *simple* answers in a world that has become so very complex; *simple* solutions for those who feel their relationships are suffering when they are overworked and overwhelmed.

The philosophies and tools I introduce are straight from the barnyard, but you don't need to step foot on a farm yourself to use them. Whether you live in a downtown high-rise, a city apartment or a suburban three-bedroom with a dog, the Archetypes and Action Plans that help all that live on the farm maintain healthy relationships and get what they want in life can work for you, too. They can work anywhere at all and at every stage of your life, from looking for your first job, feeling your way through a serious relationship or new marriage, raising a young family to growing your career over time.

Just as the people who lived on the farm planted the right seeds, cultivated, nurtured and protected them against damage, and ultimately harvested a bounty for themselves and others, you can do the same with your relationships. You can plant the seeds for better friendships, cultivate a more supportive connection with your significant other, "harvest" more willing cooperation from your kids and calm tensions at work if you understand the deeply rooted instincts that influence all of us. You can get ahead more easily on your career path if you know how to relate to your boss in a more effective, "natural" way.

Researchers have found that that successful, positive relationships with others are the #1 predictor of *human happiness*. When we look at our own day-to-day lives, many of us see relationships becoming so complicated and our time so precious, that keeping them positive and productive is getting harder and harder. Intellectually we know that we need to cultivate and nurture all of our relationships across the board, at home and at work; but frankly that sounds like a fairy tale, especially if you already hate your boss, think your coworker is a bitch or your spouse a moron. How could turning those relationships around be simple, you ask? And how can you be Happy?

By studying the happiest and most successful animals on the farm, I found that these individuals followed the same, predictable social norms and behavior patterns. They follow a simple code in relationships that produces and maintains harmony and happiness from the ground up. In the chapters that follow, the farm and its characters, with their down-to-earth rules and simple social habits, are presented as a metaphor for life in our own, more complex world. The animal Archetypes I present, in fact, reside deep within your own "inner animal!" as you make your way through life.

On the farm, I observe that an animal with positive relationships with others avoids argument or tension and thus is able to relax and enjoy life anywhere they are. They are Happy, with freedom from fear or debilitating stress. They have everything they need and the certainty that no one is out to get them. They relax and express their happiness in any number of ways. Dogs might play-wrestle with each other, cows will settle into the grass and chew their cud and horses will nicker when they're especially pleased with something or someone. Humans express their happiness in lots of ways, some obvious and many that are more subtle.

In **Harvest Your Happy**, I translated simple farm principles into a relevant, easy-to-follow guide for everyday people. I share nature's Seven Steps to Happy© and The Seven Secrets, truths that animals know and rules they follow, in order to get willing cooperation from others and live their best life. I have used the principles and methods I share in this book to help many hundreds of people who have walked through my company's doors asking to solve issues causing failure, discord, and friction in their lives. I used these techniques myself, to turn around my own life. I have built a seven-figure business from the ground up. I have a successful and happy marriage of over thirty years and live on an idyllic farm in the heart of Northern California's beautiful wine country with the life of peace and purpose I always dreamed of having—all by utilizing these secrets and methods. You can, too.

Although the information in this book can be used by everyone, it is written particularly for women who are struggling to get ahead; exhausted and stressed out by juggling work and family; trying to raise healthy, well-adjusted kids in a difficult world, or trying to keep peace at home with their husbands and at the office with their coworkers. This book reveals how, by understanding universal instincts and Nature's unwritten rules, you can make small shifts in the way you approach and perceive your closest relationships and, ultimately, Harvest Your Happy. Those small shifts help you understand and anticipate behaviors in those around you so you can cleverly redirect them to achieve the results you truly want. With this new perspective and the practical tools which I outline in this book, you can leave behind anger and frustration and calmly go about getting what you want and need at work, at home, and in relationships. You can also avoid the pitfalls on the path to your goals that so often derail success and devolve your well-intentioned determination into conflicts, misunderstandings, and struggles—dead ends for Happy.

While the subject matter is serious, you will find my writing style is intentionally breezy and conversational, like a friend talking to a friend. My hope is that you will believe what I tell you, so my message can make a positive difference in your life. Within these pages, you are welcomed into the same sacred circle of trust I have with my private clients. I know these techniques can work because they are Nature's timeless answers for more peaceful, effective living, and I see them help nearly every client that tries them. If *you* begin to understand these simple but profound concepts and put into practice the advice in this book that is built upon them, I know you can see your life become calmer, more fulfilled, and yes, Happier.

Camilla Gray-Nelson,
Dairydell Farm

INTRODUCTION

I realize the soothing power of simple life
is to find the secret of happiness.

—Mehmet Murat Ildan,

Turkish playwright, novelist, and thinker

As we all are, I am a product of my past and the sum of my experiences. I was a curious, independent child raised on a farm, spending my days exploring in quiet fascination everything and everyone around me. The animals were my closest friends. I grew to know their language, their culture, their social network. Immersed in the world of Nature, I experienced firsthand the reality of life—not the sugarcoated or hyperbolized Hollywood version of it. As a witness to failure as well as success, death as well as life, winners and losers, reward and consequence—the magnificent balance of Nature revealed itself. All things had a purpose and a place.

In **Harvest Your Happy,** I explain how the cleverest animals on the farm get what *they* want with minimal conflict and maximum happiness. The most basic animal instincts coupled with the awareness of ancient, unwritten interpersonal rules enable animals to live harmoniously together with each still getting nearly everything they want. I've discovered after years of searching, observation and experimentation, the simple truth is that humans are animals, too. Most four-legged animals manage to get along relatively easily, but they do it using tools we human animals may not even be aware of. I share these tools now with you.

So often, we know what we want from others, but in spite of our best efforts we can't get them to come around to our wishes or, worse, we ignite conflict or argument. We think we're being clear and asking for what we think is reasonable, but nothing is working. Why are they being so difficult? Why does every conversation seem to end in an argument? Why can't they see it my way or take me more seriously? Whether it's fixing a troubled marriage, raising kids that mind, getting that promotion at work, or motivating your staff to meet productivity goals in your department, when your best efforts do not work, you feel frustrated, disillusioned, angry and confused. Nothing seems to be going your way and conflict is wearing you out.

Wouldn't it be more productive and lead to a happier household if you and your husband could have a civil discussion without yelling? Think of the peace at home if your kids had more respect for you and your parental position. Imagine your potential at work if your manager was more on your side, and the time and energy you could save if your staff followed directions without resistance or without you repeatedly having to make your instructions and expectations clear.

In my present business, I am a Leadership Trainer, but from an unexpected platform. You see, I train dog owners how to lead and train their canines, using *universal* leadership skills that can be applied in their greater lives. It might be preparing for parenthood and child-rearing at home or better team-building at work or landing that dream job. The skills needed are the same, whether we are shaping the behavior of a dog or influencing behavior or decisions in a human. My unique background with animals has given me uncommon insights into who we are as human beings and where we fit in this crazy, complicated world we share. What I have learned through my experiences and personal study can change people's lives for the better, so I feel compelled to share these insights with others, especially with other women.

Why I Wrote This Book

Lord knows, there are a lot of self-help books already, especially dealing with happiness. Many of them are written by PhDs, academicians, or researchers. Why should you choose *this* book over the others? The answer is simple. This book is written by someone like *yourself*: a woman who has lived a life like you, experienced pain and loss like you, survived divorce, failed ventures and toxic work environments—like you. I have walked through the fire like you, but I found a way to avoid letting it consume me. I believe life's challenges either kill you or make you stronger. I chose the latter and I want to help you do the same.

Over years of introspection and observation on the farm, an epiphany has unfolded for me, especially in difficult times: *Life is not as complicated as it appears to be or that we have been led to believe!* The secrets of success and being happy in my life were not complex; they weren't even "modern." The secrets, it turned out, were Mother Nature's all along and were being practiced with success in the Animal World all around me. In that moment of realization, I felt like Dorothy in the final scene of *The Wizard of Oz,* when she realized, she didn't need to look any farther than her own backyard to find true happiness. The answers had been there all along. Like Dorothy, I didn't really need ruby slippers to find the secrets to Happiness in my own life. I needed only my eyes and a listening heart to receive the message being acted out by my animal mentors that were, quite literally, in my own backyard. I share with you here these secrets and how to use them in *your* daily life. You will not find them anywhere else.

I do not have a doctorate diploma on my wall; *I have something even more meaningful.* My walls are adorned with simple, heartfelt letters of gratitude from some of my over ten thousand clients over twenty-five years of work, a Woman Entrepreneur of the Year Award, many Top Woman-Owned Business Awards, and most dear to me—handwritten, personal cards from so many of my staff and clients over the years, young and old, expressing their appreciation for the life-changing lessons they have learned while working with and for me.

Today, as a result of my background, I make my living training dog owners to lead and influence their canines; but in truth, I am a philosopher and a teacher communicating a much larger message: *how to understand the motivations of others around us, how to affect change in their behavior toward us, and how to shed light on what contributes to failure and frustration in these attempts when Nature's methods are not realized or followed.*

When I work with canines, there are animals at *both* ends of the leash. I have trained well over ten thousand dogs, and nearly twice that number when it comes to the humans in families who are trying to improve their relationships with them. The more I study the dogs in my school and the cows, horses, sheep, and other animals on our farm, the more I understand my *clients*. It's fascinating to see the "animal" in the human, whether it be my clients, my staff, family, friends or in society at large. I see the raw, knee-jerk, instinctive animal behaviors in people around me as well as in every news story or current event that I read in my newsfeed, hear on podcasts, or see on television. From this broader perspective it all makes sense to me, yet I witness so much anger, angst, confusion, and sadness when the people involved are oblivious to the hidden forces that can be driving their behaviors. We only *think* we're different because we're human. Other than the number of legs we walk on, the size of our brain and the clothes we wear, for all practical purposes *we* could be dogs, horses, cows or goats for that matter. By that I mean our actions seem motivated and driven by the same deep, undeniable, and irrepressible animal instincts. That said, I believe we humans are unique in the Animal World—not because we've evolved beyond our animal instincts, but because *we have the intellectual ability to either override or capitalize* upon the instinctive forces that push our buttons and drive us as well as others around us. In my experience, however, this ability to use instinct to influence behaviors is rarely used. Sadly, most people seem unaware that they have this potentially life-changing power to control and manipulate instinct in order to improve their lives and maximize their happiness, let alone know how to do it! I intend to change that.

We can learn valuable lessons from animals in how to get along *while still getting what we want* by tapping into our and others' Inner Animal and understanding the code it follows. Animals on four legs are able to maintain harmony and achieve personal happiness amongst a diverse population, getting most of what they want regardless of their station or identity within the group. So why not us?

Get to Know Your "Inner Animal," Your Secret Ally in the Quest for Happy

When Albert Einstein said, "Look deep into Nature and you will understand everything better," he was right! If our goal is to understand the secrets of personal, soul-soothing happiness, looking deep into ourselves and there discovering our amazing similarities to animals is the first step. *It is the awareness of our shared instincts and the ability to understand and channel them, as animals do, that clears the path to harmony with others and happiness for ourselves.*

I promise you; this new perspective will change how you see yourself, your family, your friends—and your world. You will never look at life the same way again or feel powerless or victimized by it. Never again will you be just an observer in life, but one who can take control of it and find deep satisfaction in that.

Did you know that "horses feel shame, deer grieve, and goats discipline their kids" or that "ravens call their friends by name, rats regret bad choices, and butterflies choose the very best places for their children to grow up"? According to Peter Wohlleben in his groundbreaking book, *The Hidden Life of Animals,* these facts are all true. (Wohlleben, 2017) "Wow!" you say, "Animals are just like us!" My point exactly, although more accurately we could say *it is us that are quite like animals.*

Our emotions of love, grief and compassion, along with our basic survival instincts are more deeply rooted than we realize. We humans are, for all practical purposes, just animals in clothes. Just like other animals, we humans are innately selfish, defend our property, and seek pleasure over pain. We profile, bully, seek out and hoard resources and, yes, we use sex as power. Social mammals in particular self-sort into groups with leaders and followers. Human animals organize similarly into families, clubs and groups with the same characteristics or beliefs. Moreover, once humans personally identify as a member of a certain group, they are loyal to that group whether it makes sense logically to do so or not, and they can often distrust those that look different or think or act differently. It is pack loyalty first. Do not distract them with logic or facts.

When you stop trying to make sense of the human behavior, you can start learning how to peacefully influence it instead! *You can look to the Animal Kingdom for guidance in how to more cleverly proceed and further your cause in the face of any challenge.* Through the prism of this new reality, your behavior and that of your husband, kids, and coworkers will *not* be sensible or logical, so don't expect it to be. It will rarely be intellectually honest. What we do and how others react to what we do is driven not by our brain, but by our Inner Animal! Once we embrace this new reality, the behaviors of those around us finally begin to make sense and we can start to understand them. More important, once we recognize the *instincts and the unwritten rules* driving any human behavior, we can start using that knowledge to activate the animal secrets of happiness. We can use new tools to influence others calmly and effectively in our life and, at long last, receive more of what we need from them.

This current version of mankind may not be what we like or what we want or even what we hope to be as a species in the future, but it seems to be what we are today. We can continue to hope for a better mankind tomorrow, but the fact is that we need tools for successfully navigating *today's* social landscape. **Harvest Your Happy** is designed to be your road map.

Because the instincts of our Inner Animal are a force continually affecting our behaviors from the deepest level, it seems only logical to study how animals themselves manage to live together in relative peace and take some cues from them to keep our own life with others on a happier course.

From my earliest days on the farm, I studied the animals. I saw all types of personalities represented in every animal group, whether it be chickens, dogs, cows or horses. There were shy ones, bossy ones, over-reactive ones, quiet ones, friendly ones and mean ones. But the happiest ones, regardless of species, all had something in common. There was always a hierarchy, and within that working social structure, the most successful Leaders (like Bessy-Boss) went about directing others and fulfilling their personal needs one way, while the happiest Followers (like Nellie-Nice) took a decidedly different path to getting what they wanted. Bessy will be your model when it comes to more effectively getting what you want or need from others when you are in a position of *higher* status or power. Nellie, on the other hand, will be your role model with your peers or superiors.

Of course, Leaders getting what they want from others is no big surprise. What's more fascinating in the greater animal dynamic, however, is that some less important, subordinate animals still manage to get what they want in spite of the fact that they lack any real group status or power of their own. I will explain the clever yet critical techniques that can produce successful outcomes even for non-leaders as we study the example of Nellie the Dog.

While many of low rank in a group of animals are routinely denied food, resources, "things" or even space, this clever influencer and others like her today know the "secret sauce" and manage to get more. Not everything, of course, but they certainly get more of what they want and need than their not-so-clever peers. Nellie will be your inspiration in situations where you need something from another person but have no status over them.

Status, as we will see, is *situational*. Because of this, your winning strategy to get what you want will depend on your relative status to the "other" in the particular relationship or negotiation. If you are "the boss" or have higher status generally, you use one strategy; and if you are a "non-boss" or of lower status, you use another strategy. Observing this in animals was a lightbulb-moment for me. *Of course! You don't always have to be a leader or a boss or even have "power" to have influence or get what you want.* In this book, you will learn the secrets of animal leaders *and* those clever non-leaders which can empower you to get more of what you want from the two-legged animals in *your* life, regardless of the situation in which you find yourself—in the boardroom, the family room, or the bedroom! You will learn how to influence from any situational status position with far less of the resistance, pushback and argument that so often stymies us in the pursuit of our goals.

In **Harvest Your Happy,** I walk you through the process of discovering the universal "rules of the game." You will learn how to use *animal instincts* within yourself and be able to recognize these instincts in others to your advantage. With Nature's secret strategy in place, you can get more of what you want from anyone: your mate, your children, your co-workers, your staff or your manager—avoiding conflict at the same time.

Proven Methods for Life-Changing Results

I consider myself an intelligent woman and I have a lot of pride, so it is more than a little embarrassing for me to admit that I have not always done the best job with my life. I have failed and made a mess of things many times. But what I want to tell you is that I turned my own life around by using the advice in this book, and so can you.

After not one but two failed marriages and painful divorces, I did a 180 with my approach to relationships. I used the strategies I will share with you when I remarried (for the third time), and what a turnaround in my life! My husband and I just celebrated our thirty-second anniversary with a happy, loving marriage going strong.

In this book I explain the "why" behind the advice; what makes for any successful interpersonal strategy; and how to come up with your own solutions for every sort of relationship dilemma, once you know the principles. While I'm baring my soul, I will also share that I had at least four failed business ventures and endured several toxic office environments before applying the principles in this book to my present business over twenty-five years ago. Far from another failure, this company thrived from the inside out! Using my Farm-Girl approach, my business grew from a one-woman office in my pickup truck to a seven-figure dog resort and education center, complete with a large staff of happy, motivated employees and many thousands of satisfied clients. That my successful business grew primarily from word of mouth and without any dedicated advertising budget validates the truth of my message beyond any extrapolated research study.

How to Use This Book

Understanding the *Harvest Your Happy* model requires a conceptual journey that cannot be cut short. It's best not to jump ahead. The "why" behind the advice on these pages is even more critical than the advice itself. Stay with me as I take you on a journey of understanding and action. Follow the progression, with each chapter building upon the last, and try not get impatient. It's a fast and fun read.

Part One explores the theory behind the methods and my discovery of them. It begins with the introduction of the Seven Steps to Happy: The Pyramid©, a review of the Seven Secrets of Success and an introduction to the Four Archetypes and Action Styles which not only give you greater insight into the behavior of those around you but provide you a road map for the best path to reach your own goals. This section wraps up by identifying the two strategies that will always be *most* effective for you in getting what you want from others in real-life situations.

Part Two puts theory into action. We look at common, daily situations from this new perspective. You will learn what could likely be the underlying reasons behind all sorts of problem behaviors affecting your daily life and how you could solve these problems once and for all. Because of your new awareness learned in Part One, we address the root cause of problems and not just the symptoms.

I introduce my groundbreaking Pyramid with its Seven Steps to Happy. I reveal the animals' Seven Secrets and show you how to choose the best Action Styles to finally solve those difficult problems you might be experiencing with your staff, your boss, coworkers, kids and even your husband. Your effectiveness will be supercharged as you apply these new tools, and you'll find that they are applicable to all manner of situations.

I am confident these proven methods will work for you. I hope you will let the insights offered in **Harvest Your Happy** open the door to a new you and a happier life with those around you.

Let's get started.

A NOTE FROM CAMILLA

It was 1989. I had just lost my mother to a sudden and quick-moving cancer. My third (or was it my fourth?) business venture was failing, and I was on the verge of bankruptcy. All this in the wake of a second, devastating divorce just two years earlier from which I was still reeling. I was frustrated, sad, embarrassed . . . and alone.

How could this be happening to me—a smart, educated woman? People praised my indomitable entrepreneurial spirit and my "gutsiness" in the face of personal challenges. But why then, I asked myself in private, couldn't I make things work in my life?

With the world crashing in and my house of cards falling, it was, you could say, my "dark night of the soul" moment. Something had to change and that something, *clearly*, was me. Being alone in this case became a blessing, as I had many hours to think about life and the greater questions surrounding how to live it fulfilled. I walked for hours outside on my farm, in the meadows and barn. I found quiet comfort in simply watching the dogs, cows, and horses as they interacted with each other. They were lucky, I thought. Their lives were simple and happy.

Simple and happy. Those words would not leave my mind. I began to think more about the similarities between me and the animals than about our differences. We both lived in a social world of leaders and followers: those that had more and those that had less, whether it be power or things. We both felt fear, jealousy, joy, competitiveness and all the emotions surrounding our individual survival. I let my lifetime of memories with animals spread over me like a warm, familiar blanket. I began to think, if animals managed to live in peace and contented happiness with each other most of the time, why couldn't I? Might I learn from my animal friends—present and past—the secrets of living this same simple, happy life? Taking a few cues from my animal mentors, I began to change how I related to others, at work and in my personal life. Remarkably, as I reframed how I related to others, it changed how they related to me! Happy began to gradually replace disappointment and frustration, and harmony replaced friction. I was onto something, but I still pondered.

What is Happy anyway, I wondered? Does it mean you walk around 24/7 with a toothy Pollyanna grin? Does it depend on you getting that promotion you are hoping for, your kids doing their homework without complaining or your husband bringing you flowers? Absolutely not! That would be a fragile state, indeed.

Turns out our own Ultimate Happy will include not only reaching our personal goals but also the richness found in a life well-lived with others. I'll show you new ways to improve relationships with your friends, coworkers, spouse, and children.

The dictionary defines Happy as an overall feeling of pleasure or contentment. That's not the same as getting everything you want. We will always have times of joy and sadness, tragedy and triumph, frustration and satisfaction, disappointment and jubilation. Happiness supersedes all of this. Having positive relationships with others and reaching our own personal goals are important steps on the way to Happy, but happiness itself ultimately has more to do with how you put all your experiences, good and bad, into perspective and your overall attitude about life.

We can get happier with practice. Relationships take time and thoughtful action. Attitude may take time to readjust. There will be progress and setbacks even when you follow my Seven Steps, but with patience, practice and refinement, you can get better and happier. It's all about repetition and incremental progress over time.

> *We waste our time waiting for a path to appear. But it never does. Because we forget that paths are made by walking, not waiting. And we forget that there's absolutely nothing about our present circumstances that prevents us from making progress again.*
>
> —Marc and Angel Chernoff,
> *Getting Back to Happy*

It's true, not every relationship can be turned around and you may not reach all of your goals, but then no one does; and like they say, sometimes the greatest gift is an unanswered prayer.

PART ONE

STEPS, SECRETS
AND ARCHETYPES

CHAPTER ONE

SEVEN STEPS TO HAPPY: THE PYRAMID

Nature's guide to healthy relationships, personal success, and ultimate happiness

Seven Steps to Happy: The Pyramid© is the summation of my life's work—years of personal experience and study into the mysteries of behavior, influence, and productive relationships that form the foundation for your Ultimate Happy. We will go through all seven of these steps in the pages that follow. They may look simple and they may sound easy, but they are not. In fact, some may be incredibly difficult if we are set in our ways or let our egos block us.

In college I studied psychologist Abraham Maslow who, in 1943, had introduced the concept of the individual's Hierarchy of Needs. He classified and graduated these needs in a pyramid shape to clearly illustrate the progression from basic needs at the bottom (food, shelter, procreation) to more advanced needs at the top (esteem and self-actualization). He theorized that each level of need must be satisfied before the individual could be motivated to progress to the next level of the pyramid toward personal fulfillment, or "self-actualization." (Maslow, 1943, *A Theory of Human Motivation*)

I found Maslow's pyramid intriguing for conceptualizing my human psyche and life's journey ahead. However, it did not provide nitty-gritty guidance on how to get along successfully with others in my life that could pave the way for success and happiness. Though I loved the step-by-step concept of sequential needs that must be met on the way to a personal goal, I needed to learn the steps of *relationship* success that are not spelled out on Maslow's Pyramid.

For example, if I want to get to Bloomingdale's in NYC from my farm in California, I need detailed directions that take me there. I can't use a navigation system that directs me onto the major interstates but "ends route" at New York's city limits. New York's a big place. To find Bloomingdale's I need details! Guide me through the streets, down the alleys and through the busy maze of lights and traffic to my shopping paradise.

> ### Your Seven Steps to Happy
>
> - Trust
> - Situational Awareness
> - Personal boundaries
> - Acceptance
> - Reaching Goals through Influence
> - Happy with Others
> - Happy with Myself

I wish I'd had a detailed guide to point a more direct path to my personal Happy earlier on in life, so I didn't get so lost and waste so much time (and heartache) getting there. What was missing for me was a guide for living effectively and productively in a *social world, at any age*. I could have used that. I know other women could benefit, too, *so I created my own Pyramid* - Seven Steps to Happy—with the help of some unexpected mentors: the animals on my farm!

My Seven Steps to Happy Pyramid identifies Mother Nature's universal pattern of effective *social* interaction and personal effort divided into seven sequential tiers of awareness and action. My Pyramid must also be climbed in a specific order—bottom to top—each step being foundational for the next. But my Seven Steps to Happy Pyramid goes further. It illustrates the importance of creating and maintaining positive relationships with others in order to get what we want or need from them with willing cooperation . . . the bedrock which supports our own journey to Happy.

Research confirms that the #1 predictor of one's personal happiness is an abundance of healthy personal relationships. (Study on Adult Development, Harvard 1980-2010) This explains why it is not until the final Step at the top of the Happy Pyramid that we address ultimate personal happiness. Reaching Ultimate Happy at the top requires the preceding six sequential Steps which address our relationships with others.

Think about it. How is Happy even possible when frustration at the office, emotional stress at home, lack of real friends, or toxic relationships of all sorts are undermining or derailing it? When what we need or want to be "happy" in life so often depends on the willing cooperation of others, it only makes sense that my Seven Steps to Happy addresses primarily the secrets of successful relationships.

Applying the Pyramid

Happy is defined as feeling or showing pleasure or contentment. It's achieved in the Animal World only when animals follow this Pyramid's sequence of social behaviors. *Amazingly, when we apply this same sequence to our human relationships, we can harness the timeless wisdom of Mother Nature herself and we can be empowered!*

THE HAPPY PYRAMID

ULTIMATE HAPPY

7. HAPPY WITH MYSELF
I live with a positive Attitude, Gratitude and Purpose

6. HAPPY WITH OTHERS
I replace friction with cooperation

5. GETTING ALONG & REACHING GOALS
I activate my *Influence, Instinct, and Action Style*

4. ACCEPTANCE
I accept this present arrangement

3. PERSONAL BOUNDARIES
I realize the limits and expectations of my present position

2. SITUATIONAL AWARENESS
I understand my "pecking order" in this particular situation

1. TRUST
I believe in the other's character, honesty and ability

Seven Steps to Happy: The Pyramid
©2023 Camilla Gray-Nelson

Climbing the Seven Steps up the Pyramid to Happy isn't necessarily easy. To use it and its strategies will require a shift in mindset, awareness and perspective. You may have to change long-held beliefs and engrained behaviors. You may even need to disregard what you have read or been taught about relationships. You will need special skills and tools, but take heart. I have honed these myself over time with proven results, and I share them in the pages of this book.

My Seven Steps light the elusive path to harmony with those around you, making it possible to get what you want and need from them to reach your immediate goals. Besides providing the skills and tools for social success and cooperation, the Steps make possible your personal journey to Ultimate Happy which is at the very top of the Pyramid.

Composed of seven tiers or Steps, the Pyramid construction starts at the bottom with Trust, moving up through Situational Awareness, Personal Boundaries, Acceptance, Reaching Goals, being Happy with Others, Happy with Myself and finally to Ultimate Happy at the pinnacle of the Pyramid.

STEPS 1-6

Pyramid Step 1

Trust: *I believe in your character, honesty and ability.*

The level of Trust you are able to establish with someone else predicts from the get-go whether a relationship has the potential to be positive, harmonious and productive, or whether it will be fundamentally limited to one degree or another. Trust is the determinant. For example, living with a spouse that keeps secrets or has an unpredictable temper, working for a disingenuous boss, or raising a teenager that routinely lies to your face and other examples of this sort of behavior are factors which will always prevent your attaining full and complete harmony or happiness with that person—unless this behavior changes. On the other hand, when Trust exists or can be restored, a truly satisfying and productive relationship is possible. While the Pyramid and advice in this book is all about helping you achieve harmony in your personal and professional relationships, it is important to acknowledge that not all relationships can or will be perfect. If Trust is missing, try to create or restore it. If Trust is impossible, you have only two other options: Adjust your expectations for the relationship and live with it; or leave it altogether if it is so toxic as to be damaging or dangerous. Sometimes true empowerment is in our choices.

Pyramid Step 2

Situational Awareness: *I understand our "pecking order" in this particular situation.*

Some hierarchy of authority routinely forms within any group in order to set and enforce rules and expectations. This is so that the group can function safely and efficiently. A healthy hierarchy is Nature's way to avoid chaos. It prevents anarchy, the sworn enemy of group cohesiveness and harmony. It creates a structure in which each member of the group not only knows who is in charge but their own place and responsibilities within the group.

That's all pretty simple to understand and easy to accept intellectually, because we've heard it so many times that it's now part of our collective knowledge. What's not written or talked about enough, however, is that *status and hierarchy are situational.*

Relative status depends on the individuals involved in the social interaction at the time or in a particular situation. The status or power of any given individual will *change* depending on the situation at hand. A simple example would be that of a mother, who has higher status over her children at home where she is the parent. However, in the workplace where she is an employee, she has lower status than her boss. We all understand this!

Situational Awareness is not quite as obvious, however, when relating to friends, coworkers, and spouses, but it *must* be recognized and accurately acknowledged in order to avoid potential conflict and climb to the next Step. We'll sort out how to determine situational status in an upcoming chapter and the introduction of the Seven Secrets that animals know, and we should, too.

Pyramid Step 3

Personal Boundaries: *I realize the limits and expectations of my present position.*

When every member of a group knows exactly what is expected of him or her, it minimizes stress, confusion or hurt feelings. Specific duties and responsibilities for each position within the hierarchy, as well as limits to their authority, keep things calm and efficient. Personal boundaries prevent confusion and misunderstanding, two of the greatest enemies of harmony.

In Nature, once relative status in a relationship is clarified, expectations, including behavioral limitations, fall naturally into a type of order. All animals understand this but it often needs clarification for us humans. At work at least we might have an organizational chart which graphically illustrates the levels of status. Job descriptions spell out the specific duties and expectations of each company position from staffer to supervisor to manager.

When it comes to personal relationships with your spouse or partner, children or peers, however, these behavioral boundaries are not spelled out. Understanding what constitutes status naturally and how to determine yours as it relates to another person will be required to make it up this Step.

Pyramid Step 4

Acceptance: *I accept this present arrangement.*

Acceptance of our differences in abilities and status is not only the key to interpersonal harmony, but ironically, the *key to personal advancement as well.* Only from this peaceful place of Acceptance can we implement an upward strategy with maximum cooperation and minimum pushback. It is what animals know and we should, too.

9

Acceptance might come naturally to those lucky few already in a position of authority to command what they desire. Acceptance of a lower situational status position, however, may not be as easy for the rest of us, who need willing cooperation from others whom we cannot "command."

We might want more advancement at work, or greater cooperation from our spouse, but *only from a place of acceptance of the way things are now can we change the future.* Anger, argument, resentment, indignation, entitlement—all work against us, since no successful negotiation or willing cooperation happens in an atmosphere of conflict. On the other hand, Acceptance of your present position, even if you hope to change it in the future, creates a calm and rational platform for change through *cooperation!* This is where that shift in mindset might be necessary, and egos may need reining in. I didn't say this would be simple! Acceptance is hard.

If it helps, the principle of Acceptance is not a new discovery. This critical Step in our Seven Steps to Happy is a philosophy that has been taught since the most ancient of days by the deepest thinkers and practitioners. They reminded us that even water, in its flow, can go through stone if it chooses the right path. Acceptance is often your path.

Are you a boss or manager at work? If so, it might be rather easy for you to Accept that your expectations and action style will be different than those of your employees. You can Accept that you can legitimately direct an employee to do something. Likewise, if you are a parent, in a legitimate position of higher authority than your minor child at home, you are in a higher relative status position and can easily Accept that you have the responsibility for oversight and discipline.

Acceptance of different personal boundaries when it comes to friends, spouses or relationships with peers is much more difficult and complicated. In these situations, you will not be in a position to direct or demand change in their behaviors yet you must Accept it as the way

10

things must be, in order to achieve effective cooperation. Even finding fault with a peer and *telling* them to change can rock Nature's boat. These tricky relationship realities might at first be difficult to understand, and even more difficult to Accept, but we will cover them in detail in a future chapter to enable your progress up this Pyramid Step.

Pyramid Step 5

Getting Along and Reaching Goals: *I activate my Influence, Instinct and Action Style.*

With the supporting Steps of the Pyramid firmly in place, everything is now aligned for a successful *interaction*. Getting along or getting what you need from another person, be they your boss, coworker, employee, friend, child or spouse, through a productive discussion, *can* happen when approached in Nature's clever way. Whereas you may have tried and failed in the past to get results, with the preceding four Steps and the Acceptance of your real-time status in any given situation, you have created an atmosphere of mutual respect and a safe space in which even delicate conversations can take place.

At this step, if you need something from another or want to change their behavior toward you, you begin to cleverly choose your best Action approach and tap the art of influence through instinct instead of butting heads. Choosing the right Action Style will hold the answers to the cooperation you seek, and Chapter Six guides you to your best choice in any situation.

The secrets of influence that I reveal in this book involve a new understanding of the Inner Animal in all of us and the instincts that drive us and everyone else in our life at the deepest level. Holding this secret knowledge empowers you to tweak and manipulate the instincts in others to best cooperate with you. Talk about a negotiation advantage!

Pyramid Step 6

Happy with Others: *I replace friction with cooperation.*

At Pyramid Step 6, you're getting your feet wet experiencing the wonderful world of cooperation without friction. With each small success you're encouraged to keep going and trying Nature's proven technique for getting what you want by getting along.

Your relationships in all areas—family, friends, and work—are becoming less stressful and more productive. You have learned how to succeed more consistently in gaining willing cooperation from others, whether it's in getting along better with your coworkers, more effective leadership with your staff, greater admiration from your boss, getting your kids to mind without pushback, or cultivating a more loving relationship with your spouse or partner. Relationships are getting better and better, and you are achieving more of your personal and professional goals because you have replaced friction with cooperation. You are becoming Happy with Others!

Don't celebrate prematurely, however. Deep, true Happiness is still an arm's-length away. All of your work to climb the Pyramid thus far has been, in reality, to prepare you for the most important, if not the most difficult, step of all. Step 7, the final step of our Pyramid, addresses deeper issues: Attitude, Gratitude and Purpose. It is the capstone that holds the Pyramid together. In my experience, without climbing Step 7, any "Happiness" you feel at the lower levels is likely transitory and superficial . . . like *lipstick on a pig,* as we say on the farm. So pivotal is the final step of the Pyramid, it gets its own chapter!

CHAPTER TWO

STEP 7 AND BEYOND

Pyramid Step 7

Happy with Myself: *I live with a positive Attitude, Gratitude and Purpose.*

So, you've climbed the Pyramid successfully up the six preceding Steps on your quest to this final Pyramid Step 7, with its promise of your best life and your Ultimate Happy. You've evaluated each relationship in terms of Trust and the level of success you can expect accordingly. You have learned to assess each separate relationship in terms of your relative status in it and the personal boundaries within which you will need to operate. In spite of how difficult this reality might be, you have Accepted this arrangement and adopted the appropriate Action Style. You have begun getting more of what you want from others and are reaching your goals with the help of their willing cooperation, by using instinct as a tool of influence.

One might think the Happy Pyramid would stop there, at Step #6, but it does not. We are on our way to our *Ultimate* Happy, which does not end with getting everything we want, reaching our personal goals or simply being Happy with Others. Ultimate Happy is much bigger than this—much deeper. Not reaching and embracing Step 7 is like successfully navigating through a challenging Ninja Warrior course but failing the last obstacle and never reaching the winning buzzer. Missing Step #7 is why some people achieve great things in their lives but remain personally unfulfilled. There is still something "missing."

This important step turns your focus inward. It shifts your attention from achievements and relationships to youself alone. Looking at ourselves honestly is often difficult. It's easier to focus on others, what's happening around us and finding excuses in those things for why we can't seem to succeed or find contentment and fulfillment.

I have learned that the real answer lies within ourselves: in the elements of our own Attitude, Gratitude and Purpose.

The Attitude Element

"The greatest discovery of all time is that a person can change his future by merely changing his attitude."
—Oprah Winfrey

In the end, what happens in our lives is not as important as our how we choose to feel about it. We can either be a glass-half-empty pessimist, or a glass-half-full optimist. You can choose to believe your husband divorcing you for another woman is the most humiliating thing that could ever happen to you and allow it be your reason to never trust again . . . or you can see it as the Universe's gift to you—a new opportunity to find real love. And now that you know how to spot a rat.

Farm Girl Attitude

Farmers and their children know about Attitude. They cultivate it like they cultivate the land. Their brand of Attitude sustains them as it puts all of life's complicated experiences into simple perspective.

Resilience and Humility

Without resiliency, a farm cannot survive, nor the people who live on it. Things happen on the farm and in life over which we have no control. The haybarn holding the feed for the winter catches fire and burns down. The 5-star bull you invest in turns out to be sterile and you lose a whole year of herd development. Rain doesn't come. The cost of feed goes up. The price for milk goes down.

Without humility, we are prone to blaming others for our failures and never address our own shortcomings or faults which may have contributed to our bad experiences, allowing the same problems to continue. Were we really too busy or lazy to keep the dry grass mowed around that haybarn? Were we hasty or emotional with an investment decision and neglected our due diligence in checking out that bull more thoroughly? Growing up a Farm Girl, I developed my own Resilience, and later in life, my Humility.

Without Resilience, I would have crumbled in the wake of two gut-wrenching divorces and twice that many failed business ventures and resulting money problems. Resilience keeps you moving forward toward our goals, dreams and purpose. Resilience keeps you from crawling into a hole and living there, licking your wounds. It helps you hold your head high and keep going. It is Humility, however, that helps us better ourselves by realizing we are imperfect, and the world does not revolve around us. I learned Humility only after heartache and suffering.

Self-Reliance

On a farm, everyone has a job to do, and the one you are "assigned" is yours alone. No one is going to do it for you, hold your hand, coddle you, listen to you whine or make excuses. Because of this reality, Farm Girls learn to be self-reliant.

If a job requires a tractor to complete it, you learn to drive a tractor. If your animals need to be bathed and groomed before show day at the fair, you don't "hire" someone to do it for you. You do it yourself, and it makes any victory that much sweeter.

Self-Reliance creates a deeply satisfying sense of independence and power. Do you remember how it felt to get your first car or learn to change your own tire or oil? Move into your first apartment and do your own laundry instead of being dependent on your mom? When you are neither helpless nor dependent upon anyone else to accomplish your goals, it is not only productive, it is delicious.

Patience

In Nature, nothing is rushed. Everything has its season and its time. There are no quick sound bites or Twitter handles. Winter may halt the work in the fields in December, but it may be March or even April until the ground is dry enough to plow. A farmer may plant a crop in the spring, but it will not be ready to harvest until months later, in the late summer or fall. New calves take nine months to be born, and several months before their mothers can return to producing the milk that supports the farmer and their family.

In today's world of movies on demand, streaming and sound-of-light internet speeds, it's harder than ever to develop a patient attitude. Not only do we find Patience unnecessary, given today's technology, but we often *object* to things in our life that require it. This is a huge problem.

Real life and the issues we face require *time* to address and solve. Without an attitude of Patience, we expect the answers to be simple, and instantaneous. When they are not, we get mad, give up and move on. Wrong choice! If a farmer got mad and gave up when the seeds they had planted the day before did not yield a bountiful harvest the next morning, or they did not have the Patience to cultivate or nurture them, the farmer and their family would starve.

Reaching our goals, developing healthy relationships and enjoying a life well-lived is like the farm. It takes time and Patience, but the harvest is rich, rewarding, and worth it!

Respect for Nature and How Things Really Are

As fewer and fewer people actually live on farms and our lives shift to the cities and suburbs, most of us have no firsthand knowledge of how Nature works or, as I like to say, how things really *are*. Most kids get their exposure and knowledge about animals from cartoons, YouTube, G-rated movies, or visits to a petting zoo. Their parents watch hi-def documentaries that focus on the more dramatic elements of Nature: Emperor penguins on a glacier, exotic birds in flight or lions making a kill on the African plains. These are exciting and breathtaking to watch, but don't necessarily dig deep into Nature at her core or what makes her and everything within her Kingdom tick. Most people are just armchair observers.

YouTube shows adorable animals doing hilarious things which makes it easy to forget that Nature is actually complex, gritty and real. The strongest survive and the weakest perish. Slick productions that show dramatic footage of animals in conflict rarely explain the underlying causative maze of instincts and broken societal rules.

Respect for Nature and How Things Really Are means you understand the big picture and our human existence as a part of it. Fights or disagreements between animals are not unlike disagreements between people! They happen when Nature's basic rules are challenged—even unintentionally. A Respect for Nature and deeper awareness of how to avoid conflict by knowing and navigating within her rules can change your life. At the risk of getting too deep or metaphysical, realizing that everything in this life is *connected* helps everything make sense.

*"If you don't take the time to think about and analyze
your life, you'll never realize all the dots are connected."*
—Beyonce

Developing an attitude of deeper understanding of Nature and her unwritten rules that underpin how all things interrelate will be one of the secrets to your own success and Ultimate Happy!

This deeper awareness of how Nature works and "how things really are" gives us the context necessary to develop an Attitude that can take life in stride.

Nurturance

Nothing grows in a garden without nurturing. The planted seed is just the start. The seed needs to be tended, watered and fed. Weeds that spring up around it need to be removed, lest they choke out the tender growing plant. Successful relationships and reaching our personal goals and happiness in life also require an attitudinal willingness to nurture.

Once we understand what to do to improve a rocky relationship, we can't just make one grand new gesture and let it go. We must follow-through and tend whatever fragile changes that begin to emerge and not feel put-upon or inconvenienced in doing so. Whether growing a vegetable garden, a happy office or a loving marriage, your attitude of Nurturance will have an impact on your eventual success.

The first small indications of improvement in a relationship must be noticed, acknowledged and tended with the same care and thoughtfulness as the first tender shoots of a corn stalk. Surrounding factors that threaten the relationship must be cleared away. This is not a set-it-and-forget-it game. Nurturing takes time and perseverance. Just ask any parent who has spent eighteen years nurturing and raising a child. Their road to the finish line was curvy indeed with many ups and downs. Expect them in your own relationships and know they are part of the nurturing process.

Keep in mind that nurturing does not guarantee success. Sometimes in spite of your tending, watering and feeding, some plants in your garden might not make it. Not every goal you set will be achieved with the willing cooperation of others that you hoped for, even if you take all the right steps. But in the end, your ability to Nurture relationships will go a long way to reaping a bountiful harvest of personal goals.

Courage

I love the word, Courage. It may be my favorite word of all. There is something so strong and grounded and powerful about it. It's everything I want in myself, and I'm sure it's an attitude I first developed it in my Farm Girl childhood.

Life was not easy then and it's not easy now—for any of us. Courage is defined as, "the ability to do something in the face of fear." I have a wall hanging even now in my horse barn that says, "Courage is being scared to death, but getting in the saddle anyways."

I remember getting my first pony. He was quite a son-of-a-gun. I had begged and begged my father for a horse, and this was his (begrudging) surprise one day. The first time I rode Smokey he bucked me off. The second time, he ran me into the hay manger (I still have the scar). The third time, he took me under the low trees by the creek and knocked me out of the saddle. Fear started to displace my horse love. But I knew if I let fear overtake me and stopped riding Smokey, my father would give him back. So, I gathered up my young courage and got back on; and from that day forward, I was a horsewoman and still am to this day.

In that first experience, Courage overcame fear, and the result was that my confidence grew. With a courageous attitude, the seed of confidence continued to grow and has sustained me through life and all of its challenging experiences. It took Courage to leave the security of a salaried job and start my own business. It took Courage to try again, after failures. Without Courage I would never have found my wonderful

19

husband and remarried. Only with Courage would I be here today, and Courage will see *you* through the tough challenges you have ahead.

Of course, an attitude of Courage is required to make tough decisions in the face of common sense as well. On the farm, when an animal is suffering and all attempts at remedy have failed, common sense must prevail over feelings, and Courage is needed to let them go. In real life today, not all relationships can be saved, either. Whether it's a partner unwilling to commit or one that mistreats, common sense will point the way to the solution, and Courage that will get you there.

Hope and Optimism

Farmers are a special lot. Their very survival can depend on factors beyond their control. Years of drought can mean no crops and slowly drain their family's savings. Early rain can destroy a premium grape harvest in a matter of hours and with it, their income for that year. Fire can incinerate a hay barn holding several winters' worth of feed for their animals.

What keeps a farmer going on? What sustains them through year after year of uncertainty as they walk the thin line between success and failure while having no real control over either? It's their ever-present attitude of Hope and Optimism—the Hope that things can be better next time and the Optimism to believe that they will be.

Hope and Optimism were instilled in me from my parents. Some years were great on the farm. Others were clearly rocky, but my father never gave up Hope. He had unwavering Optimism and with it, was always game to try again, or try something new or innovative. His deep belief that better times were around the corner kept us going, and wouldn't you know it, they were.

Occasionally criticized for being too optimistic and too hopeful myself in the face of professional adversities, I have, in fact, used this attitude to my advantage. Not only have Hope and Optimism propelled me through the emotional peaks and valleys of entrepreneurship, but there's a full circle to this: A genuine spirit of Hope and Optimism can infuse a company and its employees—as well as one's personal relationships—with *positivity* and yes, the deepest sense of contentment and happiness.

> *"The positive thinker sees the invisible, feels the intangible, and achieves the impossible."*
> —often attributed to Winston Churchill

The Gratitude Element

> *"Gratitude unlocks the fullness of life. It turns what we have into enough, and more. It turns denial into acceptance, chaos into order, confusion to clarity. It can turn a meal into a feast, a house into a home, a stranger into a friend. Gratitude makes sense of our past, brings peace for today and creates a vision for tomorrow."*
> —Melody Beattie, American author

Do you ever look back and think, "Where has the week gone? The month? The year?" The days fly by, as we move at light speed from work and meetings to soccer games, gymnastics, and the occasional lunch with friends when we can fit it in. Who has time to even think, let alone reflect? In our rushed and over-scheduled lives, it's easier to rail against what's going wrong in a moment of frustration than taking the time to thoughtfully express gratitude for all that's going right.

I can tell you from experience that practicing Gratitude in my own crazy life was a monumental change for me. It's so easy to focus on the negative, but in most of our lives the positives far outnumber the negatives by a country mile. Many of us are blessed to have:

- A job

- Friends

- Family

- Healthy children

- A trusted partner

- A roof over our head

- Enough food to eat

- Shoes and clothes to wear

- Freedom to live as we want and be who we are

- Choices

- Opportunities

- Blue skies and fluffy clouds

- Life itself

Believe me, between leading a company, community involvement, writing books, tending livestock and pets, keeping a household and making time for my husband and marriage, I am as busy as the next person. I managed, however, to find an open pocket of time that I began using for my practice of Gratitude!

Practicing Gratitude before I get out of bed

In the morning, just after waking but before my feet hit the floor, I spend a few moments with my eyes closed, in quiet reflection. In an almost meditative state, I begin running through all that I have to be grateful for that day. Some days that's harder than others but I may start with the smallest thing, like still having great vision, while my friends are all wearing bifocals, or being fit and healthy enough to ride my horses. I am luckier than so many others in that regard!

I am grateful to finally have a good man to share my life with (even though we might be in the middle of a disagreement), who is kind and honest. That was not always the case, so I will never take that for granted. Gratitude in this case gives me perspective.

Professionally, even when there might be little kerfuffle with employees at the business, I am grateful to have a healthy business in the first place. I'll also ask for guidance at that moment, helping me to choose the right words and the right actions to make things better on that front.

I am grateful for each of my friends and think about whether I need to carve out some time for a phone call, friendly text or lunch, to keep that friendship growing, because I am so thankful to have it.

You will have your own list of things you are grateful for. Maybe my early morning Gratitude routine doesn't work for you. Maybe you're more of a journal person and want to write things down. It doesn't matter. However you do it, practice Gratitude. It is such a simple thing but trust me—it can be life-changing.

The Purpose Element

> *"True happiness is not attained through self-gratification,*
> *but through fidelity to a worthy purpose."*
> —Helen Keller

Do you have a Purpose? A cause that stirs you deeply and that you want to promote or support? Is there a greater calling that could give deeper meaning to your life and time here on Earth?

23

Often, the idea of Purpose is not on one's radar until they reach, say, their forties or even fifties and they begin to wonder what it's all been about; how they can leave the world a better place than they found it.

Don't wait for middle age to identify your own Purpose! Is it preserving the environment? Raising thoughtful, generous children who can heal a future world? Is it a local cause, like raising money to build beautiful public parks in your town or city for the generations that will follow you? Is it helping the plight of abandoned animals? Promoting the arts or music programs in your local schools or supporting the programs at your church that feed the hungry in your area?

A Purpose outside of yourself reaches an entirely different level of your awareness and humanity than do relationships or personal goals alone. Purpose gives your life *more* meaning and a source of *deeper* satisfaction. When you add it to Attitude, Gratitude, being Happy with Others, Reaching Your Goals as the result of Acceptance, Personal Boundaries and Situational Awareness and grounding it all on Trust—you can finally achieve Ultimate Happy!

CHAPTER THREE

SEVEN SECRETS OF SUCCESS

(THAT ANIMALS KNOW AND YOU SHOULD, TOO!)

Animals know things about their own actions and interactions that many of us do not, but when you read these Animal Secrets in the pages that follow, the dots of *human* behavior will start to connect in your mind! For many of my clients, it is an epiphany like no other. Suddenly, you will understand *why* your husband doesn't listen or *why* your teenager wants a tattoo or *why* gossip is rampant in your workplace.

The Seven Secrets that follow help you understand human behavior. Combined with the Seven Steps to Happy which can guide your interactions with others, will give you all the tools you need to work on creating your best life and most satisfying and fulfilling relationships.

Secret 1: Humans are animals, too!

"Some people are uncomfortable with the idea that humans belong to the same class of animals as cats and cows and raccoons. They're like the people who become successful and then don't want to be reminded of the old neighborhood."
—Phil Donahue
Media personality, writer, film producer

Apart from a bigger brain, walking upright and wearing clothes, human beings are not all that different from lower animals when it comes to behavior. There are only three Kingdoms in the natural world, after all: Animal, Vegetable and Mineral. Unless you're a vegetable or a mineral, face it—you are an animal. Granted, a more highly developed, intelligent, and capable sort of animal, but an animal, nonetheless.

Get over yourself and while you're at it, stop expecting others to be more than they are. Looking at relationships through this new lens, you will see that today's human is still influenced to a stunning degree by his/ her primal instincts, including those identical to Stone Age Homo sapiens.

Your Inner Animal

Before you can go further with the insight and advice in this book, it is imperative that you understand and embrace—beyond a shadow of a doubt—the presence and influence of the *Inner Animal* that resides within yourself and others. In fact, it seems evolutionary psychologists have peeled back the curtain on human behavior and found that what is actually controlling our grand and sophisticated human existence is nothing more than our ancient animal core—or instincts identical to it. It follows, then, that we must acknowledge the instincts that silently drive us if we ever hope to fully understand and effectively influence human behavior.

Stop Getting Angry and Start Understanding

Do you want to change how your husband responds to you, your kids respect you, or your boss or coworkers treat you? Change begins with understanding.

When some form of Homo sapiens first appeared many thousands of years ago on Africa's Savannah Plain, life was harsh and fragile. This Stone Age man, just like the lower animals, had to depend on his instincts to quickly detect and protect himself from danger. Whether it was sensing the presence of a stealthy hidden predator, feeling the drop in barometric pressure before a killer storm, or getting a "bad vibe" from a fellow dweller with evil on his mind, early man had his emotional radar up—his instincts—and he depended on those instincts to survive. Evolutionary psychologists contend that people today still use and depend on those same animal-like instincts, but of course not for the same life-and-death reasons. Yuval Noah Harari, in his best-selling book, *Sapiens,* states "We are still animals, and our physical, emotional and cognitive abilities are still shaped by our DNA. Our societies are built from the same building blocks as Neanderthal or chimpanzee societies and the more we examine these building blocks—sensations, emotions, family ties—the less difference we find between us and other apes."

Whether or not you believe that today's humans are direct descendants of Stone Age Neanderthals doesn't really matter, though. Observing human behavior today, it is clear that people *act* a lot like animals. We react first and think later. We tend to be selfish, defend property, and seek pleasure over pain. We hoard resources, use sex as power, self-sort into groups, and organize into leaders and followers. We are clearly animal by our behaviors, even if not by genes.

This first secret means everything for *you* in your real life here and now in a modern world. Any personal dealings you have with another human being—from the bedroom to the boardroom—can now be empowered with an awareness filter and the knowledge of an ever-present Inner Animal that affects their responses.

Secret 2: Instincts Rule

Intellect plays catch-up

When we understand the common instincts that subconsciously drive our Inner Animal (Angell, 1906), we can not only appreciate their importance but navigate around them or use them to our advantage. We can communicate more effectively and ultimately get what we want from others instead of running into the hidden obstacles that they can create. These instincts include:

Instinct: Avoiding the Unpleasant or Difficult:
Choosing pleasure over discomfort

Procrastinators rejoice. It's not laziness that makes you avoid difficult or uncomfortable things; it's your *instincts* that often hold you back from taking action in uncomfortable or difficult situations. The most important job from our Inner Animal's perspective is to stay alive. Because of this we are wired to instinctively avoid danger or, for that matter, any situation that feels unfamiliar or uncomfortable. Ditto for things that require lot of effort or cause stress. Both physical work and emotional stress can be exhausting. Conservation of energy is crucial for animal survival. This is why our preference, as a human animal, is usually to avoid stressful situations whenever possible.

Lower animals cannot reason themselves out of this Avoidance instinct. The human animal, on the other hand, has the ability to overcome the instinctive urge to avoid (some being better at it than others). Of course, having the ability to do something and actually doing it can be two different things.

Instinct: Grouping

We're social beings

Humans are wired to be social mammals because we survive best in groups rather than alone. Grouping is also why we pair up into couples, families, towns, and nations. It is why we have social clubs and cliques at work. The instinctive urge and need to "group up" is in our DNA and that of our family and coworkers.

Instinct: Flocking, Similarity, and Attraction

They look like me. We'll hang together!

My Dalmatians could "spot" another of their breed from blocks away and drag me in that direction for introductions. I recently realized that the majority of my own girlfriends are blonde, like me! My husband and I tend to socialize with couples that have similar hobbies and interests, political leanings or spiritual beliefs.

Why is that? Social animals are instinctively drawn to others that look like them. Scientifically, this is referred to as *Similarity Attraction Theory*. (Berscheid and Walster, 1969) (Belz, Pyritz and Boos, 2012) It makes sense as a survival mechanism, because similarity in appearance might indicate the other belongs to the same pack's gene pool—a relative that can be trusted. The instinct of Similarity Attraction is why you, your husband, kids and coworkers will flock to those with similar appearances or beliefs. It's not personal, prejudiced, or political. It's the way we're wired.

Is it any wonder that the old neighborhoods in big cities were congregations of similar ethnicities? Or that today, we are closer with those that share our political beliefs than with those who do not? There is safety and comradery in similarity. It's an ancient instinct, but Similarity Attraction still affects every one of us to some degree socially, whether we realize it or not. What we do in response to it, however, can be a matter of our conscious choice.

Instinct: Fear

Distrust of the new or unfamiliar

You may have noticed a dog that instinctively distrusts new people even though they are friendly and mean no harm. The dog barks uncontrollably, often much to the embarrassment of its owner. Compare that dog's behavior with a staff member or coworker who stubbornly resists change at work even though the change may represent an ultimate benefit for the worker. We may think their resistance is silly or illogical, but consider your own behavior when faced with the unfamiliar. Don't you, when walking alone in an unfamiliar neighborhood, get a little uneasy, especially when approached by a stranger on a dark street?

Distrust of the unfamiliar can help keep us safe, but it can also complicate relationships. Our instinctive fear of the new or unfamiliar is why we feel uncomfortable when someone we have just met gets too familiar too soon. It "feels creepy," even though you might end up the best of friends later on. Like it or not, our survival instinct to distrust anyone or anything unfamiliar is the tune to which we all tend to dance, including your husband, partner, friends, kids and coworkers.

Instinct: Classification (Profiling)

Profiling and why we make snap judgments

Animals survive through instinctive profiling, and we do it, too—not because we are inherently racist or phobic or intolerant or mean-spirited—but because we are instinctively wired to survive.

Animals in their raw and undomesticated state survive on a thin thread. They are experts at recognizing patterns and can (and must) make split-second decisions of friend or foe. If you have a pet dog, for example, he might show this ability to recognize patterns when he barks excitedly whenever you pick up his leash. He has learned that whenever you pick up his leash, a delightful walk around the neighborhood follows. He has already recognized the pattern before it happens and has predicted the outcome. In another hypothetical situation, your dog may have been attacked by a white dog with pointy ears. The first time, your dog recovered from the incident but probably had some uncertainty when he met the next white dog with pointy ears. But if he is attacked again by a white dog with pointy ears, that is a pattern and your dog will recognize it. Now he is on high alert for all white dogs with pointy ears and when one is encountered, your dog either exits stage left or goes into full self-protective mode, even if the next white dog with pointy ears is a service dog. Profiling is one of Nature's most powerful survival instincts.

Think about this next time you feel embarrassed or upset when someone you know makes a sweeping generalization about someone else. It does not necessarily mean he or she is intentionally prejudiced or bigoted or anything else mean or bad. It may just be his or her Inner Animal talking before their intellectual filter kicks in. Certainly, we do not have to accept hurtful or intolerant comments, but knowing the source helps us address them calmly and effectively. Luckily, *instinct drives behavior initially, but human intellect can override instincts when it needs to.*

Instinct: Hierarchy

Understand it at home and at work

In every group, hierarchy is the first order of business. All members of a group seem to instinctively ask, "Who is in charge here?" "How are we organized and what should my role be within this group?" In our daycare and other dog groupings at my kennel, a ballet of power redistribution occurs immediately when a new dog is introduced into the "play pack." At this moment, all play ceases and will not resume until the process of hierarchy reorganization has taken place. Even when training in a group of just two—the dog and me—we must sort out our roles before obedience can begin to happen.

Who answers to whom? It's the same in any ad hoc committee, for example, where people get together for some immediate purpose, whether it's to save the local library or organize a birthday party for the office manager. After some initial fluttering about, the most assertive and confident in the group usually starts to delineate ideas for action and ends up being appointed chairman. The chairman breaks the big goal into manageable chunks of action and asks certain people to make sure those "chunks" get done. These subleaders, in turn, recruit helpers from the rest of the group. It is this instinctive hierarchical organization of the group that allows a variety of people and personalities to work together, get along, and above all, be effective and productive. Its why Hierarchy is a basic and important instinct in most social mammals.

In families, traditional hierarchical order is pretty clear. Generally, parents are the leaders and the children the followers. For millennia, parents have assumed status and authority over their children, and their children have been shown what is expected of them. With any luck children have accepted their roles as subordinates and deferred to parental control accordingly.

This simple way of prioritizing and organizing our instinctive needs and acknowledging Hierarchy has worked as well for us as it has for other animals. That is not to say if your company embraces co-management or egalitarian groups of workers with no formally designated leader the system cannot succeed. But try as you might to make everyone in your department unnaturally "equal," you can expect either the instincts of Jealously and Rivalry to rear their ugly heads or ad hoc leaders to arise from within the group, whether or not this unofficial hierarchy is reflected on an organizational chart.

Instinct: Loss Aversion/Resource Acquisition/Guarding

Stay away from my stuff!

Parents routinely need to remind their children to not be "selfish" and to share some coveted object when tensions arise over it. And don't tell me you haven't stashed away a little secret "fun money" for yourself from time to time so your spouse couldn't claim it. The kids aren't being "bad," and neither are you. It's simply that pesky instinct to Acquire and Guard resources and things that we consider valuable. Teaching kids to share and any guilt you might feel for hiding something for yourself is just intellect playing catch-up with our instincts.

Instinct: Rivalry

Alive and well in all relationships

Any dog owner with more than one dog and any parent with multiple children can vouch for the Rivalry instinct being universal. There is Rivalry and competition for your attention, for toys, for success, and a whole host of other things. There is Rivalry between adults, too. My father had a healthy rivalry with another local dairyman for years. They were friends, but always one-upping each other in subtle and not-so-subtle ways. In one instance, his friend bought a second dairy. My father, in turn, bought two. By the end of their careers, both were the largest milk producers in our county. Certainly, it was Rivalry that helped propel each to great achievements and success in their field. This was an example of an instinct being channeled for good. As we all know, however, Rivalry channeled differently can be destructive indeed. Such is the irony of many human instincts.

It would be difficult to deny that Rivalry in humans is anything less than hardwired from our animal core, related to our relative success and most probably to our very survival. A healthy rivalry does not mean each party dislikes the other or harbors ill will. It is just instinct. When you experience Rivalry at work or in your personal life, understand the Inner Animal from which it comes, so that you can calmly work to either lessen it or harness it, instead of reacting emotionally to it. Getting mad about it won't solve anything. Understanding what's behind the Rivalry can equip you to work on the underlying causes *or use it to your advantage.*

Instinct: Jealously and Envy

They're going to happen

In its extreme form, Rivalry can morph into Jealousy and Envy. Competition on the power ladder can be fierce. Dog trainers and behavior experts routinely see cases of family dogs fighting with each other because they are envious of what the other has—to the point of conflict. These basic animal instincts of Jealousy and Envy have become familiar themes in human history, legend, and culture as well—from Cain and Abel in the Bible to the *Housewives of Beverly Hills*. Now there are some animals!

Learn to recognize natural Jealousy and Envy at home and at work. We will introduce some strategies to overcome them in *Harvest Your Happy*, Part Two.

Instinct: Curiosity and Secrecy

From withholding information to meddling in the affairs of others

Where do *these* instincts come from? They did not start with humans. They've been *animal instincts* for millennia. In animals, curiosity and secrecy are both linked to survival. Predatory animals used curiosity to investigate and locate prey. They used secrecy to hide food for later consumption. The human animal simply demonstrates curiosity and secrecy in other ways, like a child who asks too many questions or an employee who does not share valuable information.

Instinct: Shyness and Sociability

Introverts and Extroverts

Are you an extrovert that loves to socialize, married to an introvert who wants to stay home instead of going to that great party on Saturday night? Do you have one child who is outspoken and another who would rather eat glass than bring a problem to her teacher? Though it can be frustrating, these differences are instinctively hardwired. As Lady Gaga might say, they're just "born that way." Shyness and Sociability are two ends of the spectrum when it comes to instinct for social interaction. I see both extremes in dogs and we certainly see it in children and adults—those who love the spotlight, networking and joining every club they can, and those who would rather perform their own dentistry than go to a party where they don't know anyone. Again, humans have no unique claim to these instincts. They must come from a deeper animal core. Mary had a little lamb that followed her everywhere. That was a lamb with lots of Sociability. I hope Mary did not take that as proof she was irresistible. The sheep in my field, on the other hand, cannot be approached closer than thirty yards. They're wired for Shyness. Likewise, I don't take it personally. The sheep simply do not know what they're missing.

Instinct: Imitation

Monkey see, Monkey do

We all have seen imitation in our lives. In children it is prevalent as they learn new skills. In business and in industry we are inveterate imitators. Did you know that long before schools, smartphones, or even human beings, imitation was used as a means for survival? Animals imitated successful behaviors of others so that they could be successful and survive. To this day, the lioness demonstrates hunting skills for her young, teaching them to hunt as they imitate her actions. Your older dog "shows" your new puppy where to relieve himself, as the pup follows and imitates his big brother. Many animal trainers will even use a trained animal to demonstrate a new behavior when training a pupil. We Imitate because we are wired to do so at our animal core.

Think about our instinct to Imitate as you set a living example for your staff and for your children. With your kids, it is not what you say, but what you *do* that they will Imitate. At work, you will get further in encouraging behavior norms like positivity and helpfulness in your staff if you live those norms rather than just write about them. You'll see examples of how to influence through Imitation at work and at home in Part Two. Tap into the good side of Imitation and watch what happens.

Instinct: Constructiveness

Creating, building, and making things

Ants build tunnels, dogs dig dens, apes make crude tools, and humans build skyscrapers. Humans, however, are animals on the top floor of that constructiveness instinct! This instinct has quite possibly made the greatest impact on human civilization as we know it, for when the instinct to build and construct meets the boundless intellect of the human animal, astounding things happen! While ants may still be building those tunnels, humans have built not only skyscrapers but bridges, railroads, and interstates. They harnessed electricity, invented the telephone and the internet, created a digital world with smart phones and streaming video, produced medicines to prolong life and the quality of it . . . and on and on. Our drive to construct is the reason behind the incredible advancements of our human world and a vital part of each of us as individuals.

Instinct: Sex and Reproduction

The drive to survive through procreation

Let us have a little fun with this one. You might be surprised at how it changes your mind about human behavior between men and women. Not just his, but yours, too.

In the Animal World, the strongest, healthiest male in a group generally fathers most of the offspring of that group. Only the Top Dog who is smart enough, strong enough, and healthy enough to fend off competitors wins the prize. Most alpha males are large, often the largest male in the group. Physical size, then, was part of the winning equation in reproduction because it meant these males could successfully contend for the critical resources like food and territory. Is it any wonder that every man today still wants to be taller than he is? There may not be a big market for elevator shoes and lifts these days, but the next time you watch a movie, pay close attention to how Hollywood cleverly makes every leading man look as tall as possible.

There is also evidence to suggest that animal females are naturally more *attracted* to the larger, stronger, and healthier male as a useful instinct for assuring a union with the healthiest mate. Healthy offspring, after all, is vital to the continued survival of any group. A receptive female certainly makes an alpha male's pursuit much easier at any rate. No one likes to be turned down at the dance. Is it any surprise, then, that we women still find intelligence, height, and strength attractive in a man? And as far as good looks go, studies have shown that it is body symmetry and proportion that we equate to beauty and good looks. But did you realize there is a direct correlation between the "good looks" of body symmetry and health and longevity? We may dismiss our attraction to physical "beauty" as shallow in today's social environment, but the instinct to be attracted to "good looks" is deep, indeed. It may not be politically correct, logical, fair or even practical, but it is deeply rooted in the human animal.

For the animal male, reproduction with healthy females is essential for group sustainability. The strongest and healthiest male needs to choose the strongest and healthiest female. So, guess what? The females *compete* for the attractive males, and it is the healthiest, most clever, and strongest females who make it to the front of the dating line.

That is how female animals do it and we can see human parallels. Just watch a few reruns of television's *The Bachelor* for a modern example of how human females are also driven by this competitive instinct to win a top sexual partner.

Instinct: Desire to be Great or Important

Ignore this instinct at your peril

Our innate Desire to be Important (or Great) was identified as a prime human instinct in modern man, most notably by both psychoanalyst Sigmund Freud and philosopher and psychologist John Dewey. (Sigmund Freud, 1856–1939) (John Dewey, 1859–1952) It is one of the few instincts unique to man and not found in lower animals to my observation. Couple it, however, with our Grouping instinct and our need to belong and identify with a group of familiar individuals that can make us feel special, and it is easy to understand the deeper motivation behind kids joining gangs or hanging with bad friends. They can finally feel important or welcomed into a group with recognition. The Desire to be Great or Important can also supercharge our simple instinct of Competition and take it to a whole new level. The Desire to be Great or Important explains conflicts of all sorts, including problems at work and even marital dysfunction with each party striving to be "greater" or "more important" than the other.

Secret 3: We Can't All Be Top Dogs . . . and That's OK

I am often stunned by some of the current advice on how to be an effective boss, and wince when parents would rather befriend their children than lead them. "Alpha" is not a dirty word, and being Top Dog won't make others hate you if you understand what alpha really means and how it plays a central role in social structure. By the same token, being a subordinate or a "non-boss" doesn't mean you're a failure. In fact, most members of the Animal World in the majority of life situations are operating from a non-boss position, yet the four-legged animals embrace it with confidence and can enjoy a life of fulfillment and success. We can't all be Top Dogs . . . and that's OK. In fact, our differences make all the difference *because status and power differences are the secret behind social harmony!* We'll talk more about status, because it plays a central role in all social interactions, even though it may not be obvious. It is at the core of the remaining "Secrets," as well.

"Alphas" and Top Dogs Lead with Dignity

If you're the Top Dog, don't be afraid to embrace it. The alpha personality is probably not what you think it is. Hollywood has done a great job entertaining us with animals on screen, but a terrible job educating with real facts about our four-legged mentors.

Rick McIntyre, veteran wolf researcher, has studied gray wolves for over twenty years, including the wild wolves living free in Yellowstone National Park. Over time, McIntyre has noted certain "alpha" characteristics that are uniquely found in individuals who rise to the top of the group hierarchy. He has observed that the leadership role of the ranking male is not obtained by excessive force, nor through domineering or aggression. He makes the point that alpha males are not demonstrably *aggressive* by nature. They don't need to be. In fact, he says the main characteristic of an alpha male wolf is "quiet confidence and quiet self-assurance. You know what you need to do; you know what's best for your pack. You lead by example. You're very comfortable with that. You have a calming effect." (Sefina 2015, *New York Times*, "Tapping Your Inner Wolf")

Researchers also make the point that there are simultaneous male and female hierarchies in the wolf pack, with an alpha male and an alpha female. The male sees to overall safety of the pack and reproduction duties, while the female takes the lead in determining where to travel, when to rest, and when to hunt. By the way, who chose *your* family's last vacation destination? Thought so.

Leaders vs. Managers

We've long heard that leaders are born, not made. From my life of observation I agree, but *it is important to distinguish between managers and leaders.* The skills of management can be learned by almost anyone. Leaders, however, are more than managers. They inspire; they bravely lead. People are drawn to follow leaders in a sort of Pied Piper reenactment. This magnetic ability is not the product of training. Call it charisma, charm, animal magnetism or whatever you wish, but all great leaders have some form of it, and if you are born with "it," leadership will come easily to you. The rest of us must work at developing it.

Much has been written about the specific traits and skills possessed by those who have demonstrated great leadership throughout history. A familiar theme through the ages is revealed: It seems great leaders are *sociable and liked by others.* They have natural self-confidence, personally enjoy the challenges of leadership, and in many cases, feel they have a responsibility to lead. They are calmly assertive and will take action when and where necessary. From Ghandi to Churchill to Joan of Arc to Martin Luther King Jr. to memorable U.S. presidents like Kennedy, Clinton and Obama, notable leaders are bold and not afraid to face the fallout from their actions. Their focus is unparalleled, staying pragmatically on task and on message. They follow through without malice, but also without apology. Most importantly, great leaders are in control of their emotions, remaining calm and rational even in the most trying of circumstances.

Subordinates (Non-Bosses) Influence from Behind or Below

I have raised many litters of puppies through the years and noticed an amazing thing in the process. In every litter there is always a *variety* of personalities. You may have seen it in your own children. In larger families, there is often a bossy child and a timid one, and the rest with varying levels confidence in between. Why aren't they all bossy? Or all confident? Or all timid? They're from the same parents, from the same DNA and were raised in the same environment. Even so, there's usually a natural bell curve of personalities. This spread of personalities is a *good* and fortuitous thing! Too many wanting to be boss would just lead to fighting and mayhem, while all being nervous and unsure would be equally catastrophic.

Nature never intended for all of us to be the same. It's like She had her plan all along, sprinkling those-that-would-be-king (or queen) among the masses so the masses would have their leader. The "masses" of non-bosses aren't just one big homogenous group, however. They organize as well, according to *relative* power and ability on what we refer to as the Power Ladder, with its multiple rungs of situational status. The beauty of this arrangement is that Nature makes sure that everyone in a group plays a vital role with every rung important in its own way, and one need not be Top Dog to have everything they need! Anyone on the lower rungs of the ladder still has a way to get what they want and need—*if they know the hidden secrets, that is.*

The Myth That Only Leaders or the Powerful Get What They Want

It seems today's buzz word for women is "leadership." It's in the title of nearly every self-help book for professional women, a topic at every womens' seminar, and ubiquitous on social media. As if only by improving leadership skills can a woman hope to get where she wants professionally or manage to get what she wants personally? Baloney! Nature doesn't work that way, and this message and implication is not only untrue, but *unfair* to all of those women who are not and will never be "leaders." Does it mean that without "leadership skills" women are stuck and in an endless state of misery or destined to remain at the bottom of the professional heap? No!

The truth is that leadership skills and tactics only work for those in *leader* or higher-status positions. If implemented by anyone of lower situational status (the majority of us, most of the time), so-called leadership tactics can not only fail, but often backfire.

Don't get me wrong. Those in management or other leader positions, especially women, need leadership skills and tools! What's been missing in the literature and in our common conversation is the recognition and discussion that "non-boss" skills can help both women and men move *up into* leader positions at work, if that is their goal. Which brings me to another pet peeve: Not everyone wants or needs to "move up"! Who made that rule? It's caused women to feel guilty for years about choosing to be happy with where they are instead of where society or peer pressure says they should be.

The Power Ladder

"Force does not constitute right. Obedience is due only to legitimate powers."

—Jean-Jacques Rousseau,
Noted 1700s philosopher

The max occupancy on each rung of Nature's power ladder is *one*. In Nature's world, each rung of the power ladder is designed to be filled by a single, happy occupant. When each individual on the ladder has specific and separate duties and responsibilities, it prevents confusion and conflict. In fact, conflict itself will nearly always have its roots somewhere on the power ladder, and more specifically, where the ladder is unclear or ignored.

One of our most basic instincts is that of status and *status is not shared.* Hierarchy still exists in every group of two or more, differentiated on a very skinny power ladder. The rungs have room for only one.

Situational Status

Our instinctive awareness of status directs us to accept an assignment from our boss, for example, but that same instinct will cause us to bristle and take offense if an employee gives us an order. *She's "uppity." She's insubordinate.* The same thing happens when a girlfriend acts too bossy, and we have a *"Who does she think she is?"* reaction.

Why will the demand of one person be accepted but the same demand from another rejected? It's all about the subtle status in the hierarchy, your *relative status* to the other in that particular relationship or the legitimacy of that status. Your boss, for example, has legitimate higher status over you, so you easily take his/her direction. Your employees, on the other hand, do not have higher status, so you will consider them insubordinate if they try to direct *you*. Before you charge ahead and ask something of someone, know your situational status! The outcome may depend on it.

What Gives a Person "Legitimate" Status?

For status to mean anything or be useful, it must be legitimate. What do I mean by that? Wearing an "I'm the Boss" T-shirt doesn't make you one. Animals figure out their relative and legitimate status pretty simply. They don't have written contracts, job descriptions, organizational charts or titles, but there are universal factors that determine Hierarchy and who in the hierarchy has legitimate status. Factors determining legitamate status include control of critical resources, cultural norms, organizational structure, and personalities or natural abilities.

Control of Critical Resources

Throughout human as well as animal history, control of critical or important resources has been a key determinant of status legitimacy. Dominant animals control access to food (a most critical resource) until they have eaten their fill. Today, if you have two or more dogs in your household, you'll see status being acted out when the most dominant one claims all the favorite toys or treats for himself instead of sharing.

Likewise, in human history the powerful were those that controlled food, water, shelter and even basic freedoms. At one extreme, kings controlled every resource and enjoyed every freedom while at the other, slaves had no freedom and controlled no resources. It is indisputable throughout history: The more resources you control, the higher and more recognized your status; the fewer resources you control, the lower your status. In a traditional family group, we concede legitimate status to parents because they control the critical, essential resources of food, shelter, and money. Higher status is granted to employers who control our income, or landlords who control the roof over our head. Both have legitimate status over us because they control resources crucial to us. Conversely, anyone who tries to tell us what we can or cannot do but does not control anything we consider important or dear will not be taken as seriously.

Legitimate Status by Cultural Norms

Culture and tradition can also affect legitimacy. Once again, using our example of a Western family unit, children generally grant their parents legitimate status; but when this traditional norm is complicated by divorce and remarriage, we see a powerful explanation as to why stepparents get pushback. When a stepparent tries to act with authority, often the child will rebel, because they do not acknowledge the stepparent's "legitimacy."

Formal Organizational Structure

An organizational chart or a job title with job description bestows legitimate status upon individuals within a company or organization, according to their formalized position duties and their relative place on the organizational diagram, or organizational chart. Those higher on the chart (officers, directors, managers, and supervisors) with job descriptions that spell out their managerial duties have legitimate organizational status over those who appear on the chart below them, regardless of personality or natural ability.

Status by Personality or Natural Ability

In any group of two or more individuals with no formal organizational chart or contract, those with the strongest personalities and best leadership abilities often rise and take charge naturally. If the others accept this with no objection, with or without a written contract, the ad hoc leader will have legitimate status and the negotiating power that comes with it. Be careful with this, however. If more than one person in an ad hoc group wants power, in order to maintain group harmony and productivity, the group would be wise to figure out a division of duties that puts each power member on a *separate* power rung that satisfies them.

Secret 4: Beware the Conflict Twins: "Same" and "Equal"

> *"Every seeming equality conceals a hierarchy."*
> —Mason Cooley, Adjunct Professor,
> Columbia University

We have established that we may not be Top Dog in all our relationships, but that we will still have a place on the power ladder which is ours alone. Nature has wired us to expect this separation of powers instinctively, but it is also why striving to be "the same" or truly "equal" with another in terms of *power and position* in any sort of relationship will predictably rub Nature the wrong way. This is not to say that other types of human equality outside of relationships do not or should not exist, such as equal opportunities for all and equal treatment under the law; but when it comes to status and power, *it is accepting differences in power in various situations and being deferential to one another accordingly that actually keeps the peace.*

46

When the opposite occurs and someone else insists on sharing our personal status level or we assume the right to share theirs, our Inner Animals often fight to reestablish sole possession of the rung! I know that may sound odd or even shocking, but it is one of Nature's most important rules, and I see it play out on a daily basis, not just on my farm but in the news as well. "Same" and "Equal" are the Conflict Twins in all sorts of relationships when it comes to status and power.

Social mammals, as a general rule, live in groups organized on a vertical power ladder of hierarchy. Four-legged social mammals live in these well-defined societies uncomplicated by ideological or political influence, so they do just fine with this status differentiation. In our human social world, however, it can get confusing. The organizational chart at work may show we are on the same level as our coworker in the next cubicle, but we are not "equal" or uniformly the same. Modern Western society may say we are *equal* in status to our spouse, but those are just words. They don't change the instinct in our Inner Animal, which recognizes relationship status as a vertical arrangement only, not a horizontal one. *The need for subtle status differences to fill the vertical rungs of status on the power ladder is fundamental to our Inner Animal, whether we intellectually agree or not.*

This is why forcing unnatural sameness or status uniformity often creates underlying unrest and triggers conflict until this "problem" is rectified. I see it routinely in dogs who are forced to be *equal* at home, and vicious sibling rivalry ensues. I have seen it also in families with jealous, warring children, all held to the same standards of excellence regardless of ability or equally rewarded regardless of their effort. Each has been driven to confrontation by the Conflict Twins, Same and Equal, which are unable to coexist peacefully when it comes to status within the group. In fact, *understanding the Conflict Twins in real life can not only change the way we approach our relationships, but the way we see our world and what is happening in it.*

47

Secret 5: Know Your Rung

Once you've recognized your Situational Status on the power ladder in your relationship at hand, look around. Know who is above you and who is below you as well as your own place on the Power Ladder. It could be crucial in getting along with others or planning your next move. Knowing *your* rung can enable you to further identify your Personal Boundaries, reach Acceptance of your position and choose your resulting actions accordingly. *It bears repeating that Acceptance of our differences in abilities and situational status can be not only the key to interpersonal harmony but, ironically, the key to your personal advancement as well.*

Secret 6: The Negotiation Elevator Goes Up or Down, Never Sideways

Like any elevator, the negotiation elevator goes up or down—never sideways, which means you must approach every request or negotiation in a personal or business relationship from either a position of lower or higher status. The person from whom you want cooperation does not reside on the same power floor as you, so there's no "sideways" button to push on this elevator. If you need something from your employee or your child, you will ride the elevator "down" from your higher power floor to their lower one. If you need something from your boss, however, you will ride the elevator "up" to his or her power penthouse.

Secret 7: Choose the Right Shoes for the Conversation

You know your rung and you're getting ready to ride the negotiation elevator to ask for what you want. Wait! You need the right shoes! I use "shoes" as a metaphor for your Action Style. Just as you would never wear barn boots to a black-tie event or stilettos to your son's muddy soccer game, asking for what you want is not a one-style-fits-all pursuit. You will adopt a different communication "Action Style," depending on whether you are negotiating "Up" or "Down."

As we have determined, *depending on the social situation in which you find yourself,* sometimes you will be in a position of higher status, riding the negotiation elevator down, and at other times you will be lower in status, riding it up. The strategic "shoes" you choose for the conversation when you get there will depend on your *relative status* in any given situation, whether it is getting your kids to put away their toys or asking your boss for a raise.

In the first situation when you are asking your children to do something, you have legitimate status from a higher rung than they; when asking something of your boss, you are on a lower status rung. You would not use the same approach or conversation with your boss as you would with your kids; not if you want a successful and harmonious outcome, that is. It's all in the "shoes," and the shoes you choose (your Action Style of approach) must be chosen carefully to suit the situation perfectly.

Not to worry. This Farm Girl knows a winning style and can be your fashion consultant in Part Two, advising your Up and Down strategies and helping you select the perfect footwear for the ride.

CHAPTER FOUR

FOUR ARCHETYPES AND ACTION STYLES

Bessy-Boss
Ritzi-Rude
Scaredy-Cat
Nellie-Nice

I have observed that most animals *and* people, including yourself, can be roughly divided into four broad personality Archetypes which I call: Bessy-Boss, Ritzi-Rude, Scaredy-Cat and Nellie-Nice. These general personality profiles have existed through time in farm life. Believe it or not, knowing them as well as being able to selectively activate their attributes in your own social situations can help you influence the human animals you live and work with every day! Most of us are blends of one or more of these Archetypes, but usually one will most naturally take the lead in your behavior and your approach to the world around you.

Even more important than the Archetype, however, is the Action Style it represents. Regardless of the Archetype you most self-identify with, you can *choose* an Action Style of another Archetype as you encounter people and situations along the way. The Archetypes and Action Styles work in relation to others. We will choose Action Styles to *benefit* a relationship because it is the quality of your relationships that help you move up the Steps to getting along, reaching goals and your Ultimate Happy.

You'll notice that two of our four animal Archetypes are shaded and set apart from the others. These are the two Archetypes that I observe being happiest and enjoying the greatest harmony and best relationships, and we will call upon them in our own quest for Ultimate Happy as we work through the pages of this book.

Nature's Four Archetypes

Bessy-Boss	Ritzi-Rude
Quietly Fearless Leader	Emotional Over-Reactor
Scaredy-Cat	Nellie Nice
Unsure Avoider	Trustworthy Queen of Influence

The Bessy-Boss Archetype: The Quietly Fearless Leader

One of my earliest childhood memories growing up on our dairy farm was that of Bessy—one of my father's Jersey cows. She was so calm, letting me pet her and brush her—even ride her! But most importantly, Bessy was the undisputed Queen of the Herd.

Bessy was sociable and liked by her herd mates, although I would not describe her as gushingly friendly. She was calm, in control of her emotions, focused, and more than anything, she seemed to really enjoy telling the other cows what to do. She liked being in control. Curiously, the others seemed attracted to her strength and resolve.

I spent countless hours around *and on* Bessy—what else do you do when you grow up on a ranch and must pick your playmates from an assortment of farm animals? We were buds. At feeding time our ranch hand, George, would pull the tractor up to the manger and throw the hay in for the entire herd. All the young heifers and other cows would come running, crowd around the hay, and start eating. Bessy would not run to the hay. She sauntered. Why rush? She was calm, cool, and confident, almost presidential in a bovine sort of way. As she drew near the hay, the other cows would scatter, making way for Queen Bessy. If they lingered a bit too long, Bessy would drop her head and neck and give her first salvo—a low, throaty *"Moo."*

More often than not, the new girls would obediently back off. If they did not, Bessy would give a well-placed bump of her substantial shoulder to make it even more clear that she expected the newbies to move along. Only when her first two symbolic gestures of power failed would Bessy get physical, sending one or two of the offenders tumbling. Then she ate her fill. Bessy was, without question, the most powerful cow in our herd, but she achieved and maintained that rank and position *with quiet strength*, without being loud or particularly aggressive.

She did not make a habit of rattling her horns, getting in anyone's face, or engaging in daily fights with her pasture mates. It was clear she would rather not use physical brutality to intimidate. Instead, confidence, control and follow-through were her tools of choice. You may wonder how I could *ride* Bessy and not the other cows. It was not because Bessy was sweet and submissive, but because she was too *confident* to be skittish!

The Ritzi-Rude Archetype: The Emotional Over-Reactor

Conflicts between animals have the same root as our own conflicts at home and at work. Generally speaking, *conflict occurs when influencers try to be directors.* No discussion of the secrets to Happiness would be complete without a great example of what *not* to do. My Smooth Fox Terrier, Ritzi Fiona, was adorable but clueless when it came to getting along and fitting into a group. As a result, she had a hard time staying out of fights or ever getting her way. Ritzi was definitely outranked by a number of bigger, stronger and more "alpha-type" dogs in our family at that time, but she either failed to recognize that and concede her lower status or couldn't or wouldn't because of her ego.

Many terrier owners will identify with my Ritzi experience, as these dogs were bred to face down and destroy adversaries rather than commune with them. Let's just say *détente* is not generally in a terrier's vocabulary. Their feisty, reactive personalities were great for ridding farms of vermin, but often worked at odds with the social interactions expected of today's canines.

When Ritzi wanted something, she went straight for it and demanded it. Of course, because she did not possess enough status to give her legitimate right to what she was demanding, her presumptive actions were predictably met with controversy and pushback. As she persisted in her unjustified demands, her superiors would eventually get exasperated and disciplinary action would ensue, often in the form of a fight. Unfortunately, my little terrier *loved* a good kerfuffle. As a result, she developed a reputation in my pack as a troublemaker. A pain in the ass. A *doga nongrata,* if you will. She used up all of her social capital and ended up an outcast, because none of my dogs could stand her and every one of them wanted to kill her.

Ritzi was an example of a non-boss that desires a higher status, assumes they are just as important and deserving as everyone else, and falls prey to the Conflict Twins, Same and Equal. By not accepting their lower situational reality, Ritzi-Rudes rarely get what they want from others. Too entitled. Too combative. Too proud. Pursuing adversarial challenges to achieve a goal instead of fostering friendship—the only way Instincts and Nature roll for a non-boss.

The Scaredy-Cat Archetype: The Unsure Avoider

The next general archetype found in the everyday social landscape is the Scaredy-Cat. They may have great ideas but lack the guts to put them into action. They are paralyzed by a mountain of *What-Ifs*. What if I fail? What if I look foolish? What if I upset someone? What if I'm hurt? What if . . . ?

On my farm, I have a collection of feral cats. (It's our natural pest control!) To encourage the cats from straying too far on the ranch, I set out a little food inside my horse barn each day, along with fresh water and cushy blankets. When there are new kittens, I get great pleasure watching their joyous play and love nothing more than petting a purring, sleeping kitten in my lap. Some of the feral kittens are brave and tame easily, coming into the barn while I am present with just a little encouragement. There they enjoy the shelter, safety, extra food, and a lap available to them. Others, however, never get over their fear, their hesitation and their trepidation over me or other humans. Because of their extreme aversion to risk, they deny themselves the chance for a safer, easier life. Their Scaredy-Cat choices relegate them to a life within the limited and sometimes dangerous world of their familiar, instead of facing their fears and taking even a tiny chance—one that could, in fact, expand their world and improve their life and situation.

I'm sure you know some people who are limited by their own Scaredy-Cat tendencies and continue to choose the easy, but ineffective Scaredy-Cat Action Style. There's the employee with a clever new idea for increasing productivity or morale in the company but is too shy or scared to bring it to her supervisor or sits silently in the staff meeting instead of speaking up. "What if they think my idea's stupid?" Maybe it's the friend with a fantastic voice that only sings in the shower. "What if people laugh at me in public?" Or a supervisor that fails to enforce policies or deadlines with her staff. "What if it makes them dislike me?" And on and on. Scaredy-Cats and the Scaredy-Cat Action Style aren't always obvious, but they are everywhere. And so is their ineffectiveness. Scaredy-Cats rarely get what they want because they rarely ask.

The Nellie-Nice Archetype: The Trustworthy Queen of Influence

Possibly the most important and useful Archetype and Action Style is that of Nellie-Nice, the trustworthy Queen of Influence. Nellie was a member of my seven-dog pack at my home for many years. Nellie may not have been the Top Dog in our family, but she was patient, strong, and very clever. When it came to getting what she wanted from her superiors, Nellie knew something that our other dogs did not. She knew the "secret sauce" to getting what she wanted *from below*.

Nellie always looked happy and had an unusual serenity about her. She seemed content with her position—never put-upon or resentful. She never complained or felt entitled to "be in charge," yet amazingly she usually ended up with whatever she wanted! Her secret sauce? *Nellie avoided confrontation or any air of entitlement or victimhood, never vexing over what she did not have, but choosing instead to appreciate what she had and use patience and friendship to get what she wanted from those that outranked her.*

Nellie had mastered the art of getting what she wanted as a subordinate by fostering friendship and trust with her superiors. If she wanted a toy that was in the possession of a higher-ranking dog, she did not demand or fight them for it. She played the long game, being pleasant and cooperative and giving no reason to distrust or dislike her while she patiently waited for the right moment to request. This most effective subordinate or non-boss strategy involves the power of positive relationships. A subordinate or non-boss, in animal terms, cannot "demand" since they have no real power or authority to do so. They either take what's given to them or they figure out a different way to get what they want that does not require power or status. Nellie's strategy can be the blueprint for your own behavior when you need something from someone with higher status or more power. She is your mentor in situations where you want something from someone but have no clear status or leverage over them in the negotiation.

Statistically, there will always be more subordinates than leaders in any social group. More worker bees than queens. But as I referenced earlier, some subordinates in this massive pool are better than others at getting what they want without the benefit of status on their side. They manage to get a few *more* resources than their counterparts and in doing so, they elevate and improve their lives.

What's Nature's secret for getting what you want if you're not the boss? *Stop complaining or being demanding and just be nice.* Sometimes I wonder if Dale Carnegie consulted with a dog like Nellie before he wrote his iconic book, *How to Win Friends and Influence People?* (Carnegie, 1936)

Remember, those who have more power or higher status than you are controlled as much by their Inner Animal as they are by their intellect, and that can work to your advantage, as Nellie knew so well. She avoided behaviors that would trigger Anger, Jealousy, Resource Guarding or Competition, and instead made sure her actions complemented others' instincts for Group Cohesiveness, their Desire to be Important, etc.

Among humans, all four of our basic Archetypes are alive and well. Think of how you routinely see and hear, for example, people in the news being Ritzi-Rude. They over-react, bully, shout, and threaten. They make you mad. You don't trust or respect them. You probably wouldn't go out of your way to do them a favor or give them the benefit of a doubt.

By contrast, I think of my best friend as well as my favorite riding horse. Both of them are Nellie-Nice! Neither my friend nor my horse would think of being snappy or unpleasant with me. They just enjoy getting along. Every interaction with them is easy and fun, and I'd do *anything* for either one of them. Not because I'd have to, but because I'd *want* to.

When you can see the *Archetype* in people, understand their actions, and recognize the instincts driving not only their behaviors but the reactions to them by others, it all begins to make sense. You will never look at the world the same way again!

CHAPTER FIVE

BESSY-DOWN AND NELLIE-UP:

TWO STRATEGIES TO MAKE
OTHERS SIT UP AND BEG

Now that you know the Four Archetypes, it is time to learn how to apply their Action Styles to situations you encounter in Pyramid Step 5. What this means for *you* is that, regardless of the Archetype that reflects your own natural personality type, you can strategically choose another Archetype and Action Style when it comes to approaching someone for what you want or what you'd like them to do. In most (possibly all) situations, you must *act* in either a Bessy-Boss or Nellie-Nice fashion or be prepared to kiss your desired outcome goodbye. Leave Ritzi-Rude and Scaredy-Cat in the back of the closet, along with the shoes that hurt your feet and the pants that make you look fat.

I'll give you simple guidelines for when to choose Bessy or Nellie as your *Action* mentor. Let us start by studying the Bessy-Boss Action Style and how she uses her higher status to get what she wants from others, willingly.

Bessy-Down

The "Bessy-Down" Method of Directing from the Top

*"Leadership is the art of getting someone else to do
something you want done because he wants to do it."*
—Dwight D. Eisenhower,
*5-Star General and 34th President
of the United States*

Besides being naturally confident and self-assured, Bessy the cow had a particular way about her and a way of interacting with her herd mates that should be a model for all of us in a position of power or leadership. Bessy's strength drew others to her like a magnet. We could always tell where Bessy was in the field. We just looked for the biggest group of cows and there she would be, right in the middle of her adoring followers. She had her own fan club! I think you could safely say her staff loved her.

How Bessy Got Her Status

One of Bessy's secrets was that she instinctively knew that without follow-through, there are no rules and no power. Actions without consequences open the door to anarchy, where actions grow out of control. Bessy gave clear signals about her rules and expectations and consistently followed through to enforce them. Because the herd respected Bessy, understood her rules as well as the consequences for not following them, they complied without argument or resentment. Most importantly, Bessy was never truly angry and didn't make consequences personal. She was pragmatic. She had no "enemies" and because of this, when her rules were followed, she was a happy member of the herd and they, happy herdsters alongside her.

Bessy's Fearless Follow-Through Model

Bessy's effectiveness came from her willingness and ability to follow through and enforce her rules in a fair and respectful manner. She did this by employing a consistent, three-stage discipline model, which would escalate slowly from gentle reminder to serious consequence as necessary. (It usually wasn't.) We can take our cues for following through with the humans

- Give a subtle reminder or warning
- Formalize disapproval and clarify expectations for change
- Take serious action if expectations are not met

over which we have legitimate authority in our life from Bessy, whether it be with our staff or employees at work or our children at home. We have legitimate status over both, so we can channel the Bessy-Boss Archetype.

Give a subtle reminder or warning

At the first sign of a subordinate's poor performance, Bessy would give a subtle reminder or warning—maybe a lowered head and a grumbling moo—to indicate that the subordinate's behavior was less than acceptable at that point. It was her way of letting a subordinate know early on that they needed to quickly change course and improve, rather than letting things devolve irreconcilably. I think you could say that Bessy's subtle early warning was Nature's version of a critical, well-timed performance review. In either case, the subordinate is being treated fairly and given the dignity of an opportunity to voluntarily improve.

Formalize disapproval and clarify expectations for change

If her subtle warning was not heeded, Bessy got more direct. She might give a louder verbalization and step into the subordinate's space so that there was no doubt that she was displeased. No one could misread or misunderstand her actions because they were no longer subtle. Those who had misbehaved accidentally or out of ignorance quickly shaped up. Only those who intended to challenge Bessy would ignore this formalized disapproval and her clarified expectations. This was Bessy's version of being called into the boss's office and having a record put in your employee file, or being asked by your mom, "Are you going to fix this or do you want me to tell your father?"

Take serious action if expectations are not met

In the case of true insubordination and defiance in spite of all the chances she had given for compliance, Bessy would finally step it up to physical consequence. Her eyes went steely, and her determination and purpose were palpable. Without hesitation (or anger) she got serious. For a cow, that might be ramming the offender off their feet, repeatedly, if necessary, until they left the scene in defeat. As they walked away, Bessy would stand quietly as if to say, "I hope you learned from this." In a workplace application, a final follow-through step *Bessy-style* might be suspension, leave without pay, or termination. At home with kids, it could be restriction or suspension of favorite activities.

In the end, it is calm and fair follow-through that can legitimize your situational status and earn the respect of your staff or your children. Bessy-Boss can direct, motivate and enforce all at once, without losing her cool or the respect of others. She is loved, not feared, and for most, she is their hero.

Understanding What Causes Ineffective Leadership without a "Bessy-Down" Strategy

In my own experience and observation, I see many leadership failures due to timidity, lack of confidence, and failure to follow through. Many in positions of legitimate authority (at home or at work) adopt either the combative Ritzi-Rude, the laid-back Nellie-Nice, or the timid Scaredy-Cat Action Style instead of channeling the more appropriate style of Bessy-Boss. Granted, it is more difficult to lead like Bessy if your innate personality is not like her, but effective leadership and direction is embodied by Bessy's style and Bessy's only.

Nellie-Up

The "Nellie-Up" Method of Influencing from Below

> *"Constant kindness can accomplish much. As the sun makes ice melt, kindness causes misunderstanding, mistrust, and hostility to evaporate."*
> —Albert Schweitzer, Nobel Peace Prize, 1952

Nellie, as you remember, was not Top Dog, but neither was she on the bottom rung. Still, those toys and other enviable goodies which were all controlled by the boss dog were things she wanted to enjoy, too. How she got what she wanted is a model for all of us who want things we may not be entitled to demand in our current situation, but desire just the same.

- Requesting, not demanding

- Fostering friendship and trust

- No ego or entitlement

63

The New York Times bestselling book, *Quiet: The Power of Introverts in a World That Can't Stop Talking*, validates what Nellie knew all along: Being effective can take many forms, including quiet influence. Nellie was an expert at earning the Trust of her superiors, and her secret weapon was being just plain easy to like. She always seemed to be happy and had a comfortable ease about her. It was impossible to dislike Nellie. She had low status, but no insecurities. She knew exactly what she wanted and how to get it. Such a smart, clever girl! Nellie was the most perfect example of how to get what you want from others of higher status through cleverer Influence, and why an entire archetype bears her name.

Requesting, not demanding

Being lower on the food chain than a Bessy, a Nellie cannot demand or just *take* what she wants. She can only request it. Wise Nellies know that the secret of getting what they want, without high status, is willing cooperation from their superiors or peers. To request is always more effective than to demand.

Fostering friendship and Trust

Nellies realize that cooperation from others over which they have no legitimate power springs from friendship and trust. As an ally instead of a rival, they are far more likely to be granted their requests, as it is Nature's way to be generous with those we like and trust.

No ego or entitlement

There can be no ego or sense of "I-deserve-this" entitlement in a Nellie's approach to relationships. This might sound simple, but it can be quite difficult when, for example, someone with an innate Bessy-type personality and a strong ego must assume a Nellie-Up approach when discussing a possible raise or a difference of opinion with her boss. Nellies spend their time developing friendships and building alliances.

For a Nellie, It's Really about Their Bessy's Generosity

The Bessy's of the world get what they want by directive; Nellies can't legitimately tell their Bessy's what to do, so they get what they want through the tolerance and generosity of their Bessy. They earn this tolerance and generosity by being easy to like, cooperative, and fostering friendship and cooperation in order to be most advantageously regarded by their Bessy. The granting of a Nellie's request is not because they demand it; it is because Bessy *wants* to give it to them—because she likes and trusts them.

Is it any surprise that countless modern studies in reciprocity, including those by today's leading persuasion expert, Robert Cialdini, confirm what clever animals have known all along: that if you do something nice for someone first, they are more likely to reciprocate? In fact, one of the cornerstone principles in Cialdini's bestselling book, *Influence: The Psychology of Persuasion,* is reciprocity. (Cialdini, 1984) It means, in short, if you want to influence someone, get them to like you first. I would say it this way: To get what you want from your Bessy-Boss, be Nellie-Nice!

As a Nellie in certain situations, you can get more of what you want *not* because your Bessy owes you anything, but because they *like and trust you.* Remember that Trust is the ground-level Step of our Happy Pyramid, and nowhere else is it clearer than in your Nellie-Up strategy. In a Nellie-Up relationship, your Bessy does not "owe" you anything. She or he will give it only to one they trust and consider a friend.

Notice that I did not say you need to *see* yourself as subordinate in order to employ "Nellie-Up" as your get-what-you-want Action strategy. It's simply that status rungs are never really shared, so if you aren't Bessy, then you *must* be Nellie. You may hear "Same" and "Equal," the Conflict Twins, screaming at this and calling your name; but tell them to get lost, because there is no such thing as "equals" when it comes to situational status, and you don't want the fight they bring!

Over time, as you take on your Nellie role and Action Style with anyone whose situational status is higher than your own, you will no longer be seen as their opponent but someone more trusted: an ally, if you will. To put it bluntly, with a Nellie-Nice Action Style you become easier to like, and this will be crucial when getting what you want or achieving influence over those with more or equal power than yourself. Put your ego aside and realize the simple truth that all of us are more generous and cooperative with people we like than with those we do not.

It really is that simple.

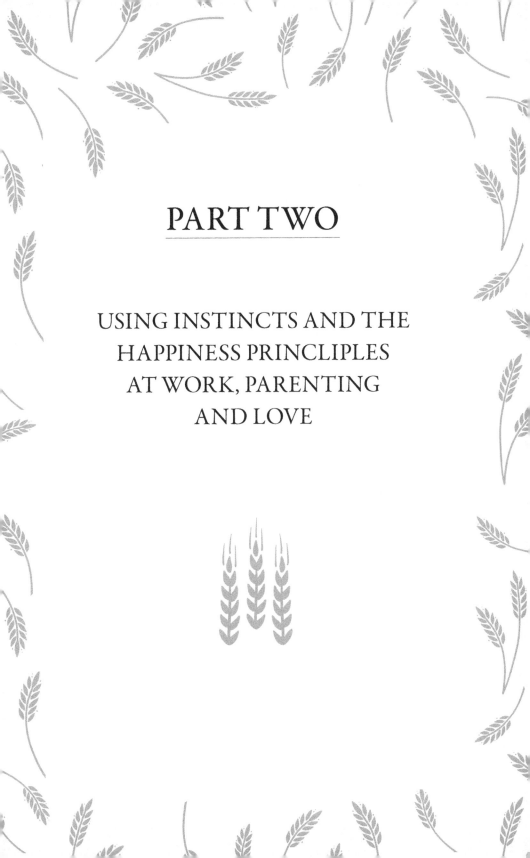

PART TWO

USING INSTINCTS AND THE
HAPPINESS PRINCLIPLES
AT WORK, PARENTING
AND LOVE

CHAPTER SIX

ARE YOU A BESSY OR A NELLIE? IT DEPENDS

Now it's time to *apply* all the new tools in *Harvest Your Happy*. The sample scenarios here in Part Two come from my personal experiences and those of my clients and friends who have used the principles in this book to change their lives for the better. I chose these particular examples because they are universal, and some may even be familiar to you. In each scenario I help you understand what can really be going on at the deeper level with the individuals involved, caution you on what to avoid, and show you how to select the appropriate tools to restore necessary harmony, rebuild relationships and get what you want, whether it's in the workplace, with your children or at home with your significant other.

Remember in your tool bag you have the Seven Secrets, Seven Steps and Four Archetypes, *but only two effective Action Styles* from which to choose for healthy relationships and ultimate Happiness: Bessy-Down or Nellie-Up. I will guide your selections.

You will notice that in every situation at work and at home, almost everything relates back to relative status and who controls more critical resources because in the end, that is how status is determined universally in the Animal World. Knowing who controls critical resources in any given interaction is what is meant by Situational Awareness, found on our Happy Pyramid.

Here is a handy guide to quickly determine your negotiation status and corresponding Action Archetype in these common situations:

Work

• Use "Nellie-Up" with Your Boss.

If you need your job, and your boss has the power to hire and fire, it is pretty obvious that "Nellie-Up" is your best Action Style. A source of reliable income is a critical resource and your boss controls it.

• Use "Bessy-Down" with Your Staff.

You are in the power position if you are a supervisor, manager, or director with staff that report to you. It is you with the power to hire or fire, promote, grant raises, or at least make recommendations to that effect.

You control those critical resources of the workplace for those that report to you. From this position of legitimate status, you can skillfully employ your "Bessy-Down" Action Style, to effectively lead and get results without dictatorial or otherwise over-aggressive tactics.

• Use "Nellie-Up" with Your Coworkers.

Regardless of your vast experience, superior skill, or higher intelligence, you have no organizational status over any of your coworkers—even the newbies or the slackers. Unless you have formal supervisory or managerial authority, leave the critique of your coworkers to their boss. You will get better results without pushback by being Nellie-Nice and adopting a "Nellie-Up" Action Style. Cooperation and a productive relationship start with you being *liked* by your coworkers. Treating others like you would wish to be treated is not only the best way to inspire a team to action, but the best antidote to a toxic workplace. There are no toxic packs or herds in Nature. Think about it.

Parent/Child Relationships

Are you the parent of your minor child and do you provide their food and shelter?

- **If so, use "Bessy-Down."**

There are no resources more critical than food and shelter. If you are your child's major source of these resources, you have legitimate status over them and can direct them accordingly.

Does your adult child live in your home?

- **If so, use "Bessy-Down."**

Again, even if your child is an adult, *you* control their shelter—a critical life resource. It doesn't matter if they are paying rent. Unless or until they move out, you are providing shelter, so this gives you legitimate higher status.

Is your adult child entirely self-sufficient, living elsewhere, and paying for their own shelter, food and "stuff"?

- **If so, use "Nellie-Up."**

In this case, you do not control any of your child's critical resources. You do not control their money or their shelter or their food. They control them. Get off their back, be supportive and friendly, give advice instead of direction and then let the chips fall where they may. When you stop telling your adult child what to do without the status to justify your directives, they may eventually start doing what you suggest on their own, because they stop thinking of you as a nag and start liking you again. Being liked and trusted is how "Nellie-Up" works.

Are you paying for your adult child's education?

- **If so, use "Bessy-Down."**

If getting an education is considered a critical resource and you are paying for it, you've got the status card here and can legitimately play it when necessary.

Are you a minor child or young adult living at home or otherwise considered a "dependent"?

- **If so, use "Nellie-Up."**

Being a dependent simply means you are "dependent" on someone else for critical resources like shelter or money or food or some combination of same. You are not in a position of higher status than the provider of these resources, so best to go "Nellie-Up" when asking for anything.

Marriage and Personal Relationships

Have you and your spouse or partner formally agreed that *you* have the final say in all decisions?

- **If this is truly the case, use "Bessy-Down."**

Be careful here, however. Even though you and your spouse have agreed intellectually to your higher status in all situations, use your "Bessy-Down" strategy with sensitivity. Remember that Bessy is fair, reasonable, and friendly.

Have you and your spouse/partner formally agreed that *they* have the final say in all decisions?

- **If so, use "Nellie-Up."**

In this scenario, you've agreed with your mate that they will have the final say in case of a tie. Status in this case is not related so much to resources, but to a formal agreement between parties. This agreement has tacitly placed you in the Nellie-Up position. There will be situations, however, as you go through life together that you will really want your way and may even regret your "they're-the-boss" agreement, but take heart! "Nellie-Up" is not only the arrangement you have agreed to, but in my experience, it is the strategy that works best in *every* marriage arrangement.

Have you and your spouse formally agreed that your joint decisions will be by *mutual* consent?

- **If so, use "Nellie-Up."**

You've agreed that no one is "the boss" but that you two will reach important decisions by joint consensus. Sounds so easy, right? Just remember, in a relationship of shared responsibilities and shared effort, "Bessy-Down" demands are off the table. You have agreed that no one would be "the boss," so don't act like one! If you start making demands on your spouse with an ill-chosen "Bessy-Down" approach, there may be resentment, competition, and conflict.

A "Nellie-Up" negotiation strategy, on the other hand, will not only foster the partnership you envision in marriage but will make you and your spouse better friends. As trustworthy friends, each of you will be more generous to the other. Remember the power of reciprocity!

Have you and your spouse or partner *never formally discussed* who would have the final say in your relationship?

- **If so, use "Nellie-Up."**

See above! You haven't agreed to be "equals," but neither have you agreed that anyone would be Top Dog. If your resources are shared and no one has been ordained the formal boss of them, then your only smart choice is to relate in "Nellie-Up" fashion. Be friends. Be respectful of each other's opinions and ideas. Be supportive. Ask for what you want, but do not demand it. You will be surprised how much you get when you stop rubbing someone's Inner Animal the wrong way. To sum it up, only the individual of "higher situational status" in a given social scenario can legitimately impose their will on another or direct downward. Everyone else must *influence upward* if relationship harmony is to be preserved and desires fulfilled. It is Down or Up—Across is not an option.

In our human societies, we may rightfully expect equal opportunity, equal respect, and equal treatment under the law, but we cannot expect equal *authority* without pushback and conflict. The rungs on Nature's power ladder have a maximum occupancy of one at a time, but we can still effectively get what we want in life despite that truth. *Our status in a social scenario or hierarchy should merely determine our Action Plan—not our fate.*

Alphas and Top Dogs are the sexy role models that receive most of the attention when it comes to advice for success, but I assure you they are not always the best models for getting what you want, unless you hold the rare position of higher status. More often than not, your Action Style for success will be the one less expected. At the end of the day *all things are possible for all of us*—if we choose our strategy wisely and go after them in the right way.

CHAPTER SEVEN

HOW TO SURVIVE
THE OFFICE PACK

*"I am not afraid of an army of lions led by a sheep;
I am afraid of an army of sheep led by a lion."*
—Alexander the Great

Bessy-Down

If you are in a position of recognized organizational power—a supervisor, manager, director or executive—you are in a legitimate leadership role. You *are* Bessy-Boss. How closely you adhere to a Bessy-Down Action Style as you lead may well determine if your staff follows you willingly. Understanding the true nature of leadership, what motivates your staff and what drives their behavior at the instinctive level will help you solve many types of issues that may be poisoning your workplace and in turn gain the respect and admiration of your subordinates. This understanding can allow you to inspire your staff to take your direction more willingly and start achieving your management goals as a result.

My advice is that your Action Style always be "Bessy-Down" with staff. Your status as boss is legitimate, but your staff may need help with

Steps 3 and 4 of the Happy Pyramid: Personal Boundaries (management's expectations) and Acceptance (of their own roles and responsibilities).

Good leaders make expectations of Personal Boundaries clear and attainable. Aggressive, strong-arm management can predictably result in staff pushback or resentment, but a carefully crafted Bessy-Boss leadership style can help assure your employees' Acceptance of their responsibilities as well as affirming your management role and status position.

Following though in your Bessy-Boss Action Style is most important. Demonstrating your ability to enforce rules and stop unwanted behaviors in others is what can create and maintain status advantage. It's the same in the animal world. Animal leaders are the ones that enforce rules. As you lead through issues with unwanted behaviors, use Bessy's Fearless Follow-Through *respectfully,* beginning with a reminder and subtle warning, then formalizing the problem, spelling out expectations for change, and finally more serious disciplinary action if expectations are not met. Remember, without enforcement rules are just "suggestions."

By giving every opportunity for the offending employee to save face and turn their behavior around quickly, you manage to be nice while still being the "boss," the hallmark of a winning Bessy leadership style.

Your Bessy-Down Action Guidelines with Workplace Staff

Put these leadership guidelines on your bathroom mirror (alongside your Happy Pyramid), on your desk, inside your notebook at work or any other place for easy reference as needed.

- Stay calm and laser-focused on the matter at hand.

- Don't over-react.

- Don't get distracted from the message.

- Believe you're the boss and act with dignity.

- Make your rules clear and consistent.

- Don't beat around the bush.

- Don't fidget or act uncertain.

- Look subordinates in the eye.

- Follow through and enforce rules without anger or apology.

- Don't be afraid to consequence for broken rules.

- Be nice while still being the boss.

I encourage you to add some of the following techniques to activate cooperation *instincts* in your staff:

- Use praise and feedback.

- Outline a reward system.

- Allow mastery by assigning certain responsibilities.

- Encourage frequent group interactions.

By making these small changes, you can tap into the *positive* side of your staff's deepest instincts. Let's tackle some real-life situations that managers often face in the workplace, using what we've learned.

Situation: Not Following Directions or Company Policies

You have a dress code at work. Company policy states employees must wear closed-toe shoes (for safety reasons) and solid-tone clothing in company colors (to avoid the need for uniforms.) You notice that more and more your staff are coming to work in sandals and Hawaiian shirts.

Understand It:

Not following directions or company policies happens when it is "easy" to do so. In this particular case, a dress code policy has been written but not enforced, so avoiding the dress code has not been difficult. It has become "easy." Given the opportunity, our Inner Animal will always choose easy over difficult, just as we choose pleasure over discomfort. An employee choosing easy is not necessarily lazy. In truth, choosing the easiest option is how our Inner Animal instinctively conserves energy and survives. The important thing for managers, however, is that easy and difficult are relative. *What is easy and what is difficult will depend on how the boundaries of acceptable and unacceptable behaviors are drawn and enforced by the manager.*

Sometimes not following company rules can have another source: testing or challenging the Hierarchy. Acceptance of the existing hierarchical arrangement is what keeps peace on the farm and is one of the key building blocks in our own Happy Pyramid. However, our Inner Animal must be certain that leaders are really leaders before it agrees to follow them.

Testing and challenge can take many forms at work. Some individuals will directly defy; others just stop responding in a form of passive-aggressive behavior. Don't take it personally if you are the one in charge. The solution again lies in *follow-through, the proof of power.*

Bessy's Fearless Follow-Through is the model for this type of skillful and leader-worthy action.

Avoid Ritzi-Rude, Scaredy-Cat and Nellie-Nice:

Don't go all Ritzi-Rude and get angry with your staff for ignoring policies. Their Inner Animal will not follow one who is perceived as an "emotionally unstable" leader. Visible anger or frustration reads as emotional instability and will be detrimental to effective leadership. Keep your cool and your Ritzi-Rude in check!

If you take the Scaredy-Cat route, however, you are allowing problems to continue rather than bringing up the issue at hand and risking someone not liking you. I have yet to see company policies spontaneously reestablish themselves in the workplace, so forget a Scaredy-Cat Action Style. It will be futile in affecting change and getting your staff back on track.

Likewise, avoid a Nellie-Nice Action Style. As the *boss*, your job is not to accommodate staff who are failing to follow policy. Your job is to enforce the company rules. Nellie-Nice is a *subordinate's* Action Style, not a leader's.

Take Action with Bessy-Down:

Get your Bessy on! A Bessy knows that a leader's greatest responsibility is not to threaten, intimidate, or force compliance. It is to set clear rules and boundaries, and once delineated, enforce them with thoughtful follow-through. This approach can give any leader clarity and power. *Clear rules and boundaries not only resolve issues quickly but also prevent problems from happening in the first place, making conflict ultimately unnecessary.* It is one of the greatest truths in management and the secret that every great leader knows, especially a Bessy-Boss.

Effective leaders make great choices easy and attractive, and the bad choices less appealing and more difficult to make. My own goal as a leader is always to praise employees for great choices rather than criticize them for bad ones. I key into their Desire to be Great, and in my experience, instinct-savvy motivation has often been more effective in changing an employee's behavior than criticism. It's my own secret sauce!

Another reason employees disrespect company rules or policies may be disinterest. They don't feel *connected* to the company or department through their Grouping instinct. In this case, you might add something to their duties that makes their job overall more challenging or satisfying. Think about their instinctive Desire to be Great or Important in front of their peers. Is the employee into photography? Consider making them the official photographer at your next company get-together. If they are the meticulously organized type, you could give them a special project for reorganizing the supply room. Perhaps they are naturally artistic. Putting them in charge of redecorating the break room could be just what they need to start feeling important and more valued within the group.

While you are making employees' jobs more rewarding, don't forget to explain the "why" behind the company policies. You'll be amazed at how simply a deeper understanding of the reasons behind company rules and policies can create greater Acceptance and cooperation. For example, our front office staff is expected to pick up a call by the third ring. When we notice someone letting the phone ring longer, we find a good time to talk in private and explain that our third ring policy exists *because it tells the customer that they are important.*

We require clean, pressed uniforms company-wide. If someone consistently shows up for work in wrinkled clothing or out of uniform, our conversation with them does not just remind them of the policy they failed to follow but explains the "why" behind the policy. We explain that our dress code is intended to communicate our company's attention to detail, reassuring the client that we run a clean and organized business and will also give the same sort of careful attention to their dog if they stay with us.

Once an employee understands and embraces company policies and rules, he or she can feel a stronger Grouping/Belonging instinct and as a result, be more likely to behave in a way that *supports* the group (following policies) rather than fractures it (not following them).

Situation: Failure to Complete Tasks or Meet Deadlines

The office manager in your small business is in charge of writing your Facebook posts. He is supposed to do four posts per month, but he rarely does. You wonder whether he would get them done at all if you weren't constantly reminding him.

Understand It:

Meeting deadlines is always stressful. This situation is complicated because our Inner Animal instinctively tries to avoid stress whenever possible. Missed deadlines aren't necessarily because your staff is lazy, but when deadlines are not enforced or there is no consequence for missing them, they are mere suggestions and meeting them just a stressful option to be avoided.

Another reason assigned tasks and deadlines are not being met could be found within the Pyramid itself, specifically in the Acceptance Step. Remember that our Inner Animal is reluctant to take orders from anyone we do not *believe* is higher in rank. Organizational charts or diagrams on paper notwithstanding, situational status is a matter of *perception* to our Inner Animal, and when it comes to our instincts, perception is reality. Does this employee truly believe in your higher authority and fully Accept his role as subordinate?

Avoid Ritzi-Rude, Scaredy-Cat and Nellie-Nice:

I know we tend to think that spelling out an assignment or expectation once should be enough. We might feel justified to act in a Ritzi-Rude fashion as we get upset when the expectation is not met, or the assignment is not completed as specified. After all, we tell ourselves, we had been clear and now we feel within our rights to be perturbed. Unfortunately, if your Ritzi-Rude Action Style rears her ugly head with anger, intimidation, or accusations, the result could lead to a combative relationship rather than a cooperative one. Need we even talk about the ineffectiveness of a Scaredy-Cat approach to solving the management problem of missed deadlines or any other compliance issues, for that matter? A Scaredy-Cat manager is likely doomed to a career of frustration and ineffective leadership because few subordinates take them seriously. No guts, no glory.

By the same token, managers adopting a Nellie-Up Action Style only suggest compliance rather than enforcing or requiring it and by doing so, are casting themselves in a subordinate role.

Remember that Nellie-Up is a strategy to get what we want from others who are *higher* in rank than us. No manager can expect to be taken seriously if their Action Style that lacks enforcement indirectly suggests they are subordinate to their employees. This is a job for Bessy-Boss!

Take Action with Bessy-Down:

The Bessy-Boss Archetype is not only strong, principled and focused, but fair and friendly and understands how to influence through instinct instead of brute force. When a Bessy needs to enforce and follow through, they do it in Bessy's Fearless Follow-Through way. They are unafraid and acutely aware of the instincts that may be involved and what makes others tick, including what can create *motivation* from the deepest level.

I came across an example of instinct-savvy advice several years ago on Entrepreneur.com. According to the article, a company called Eastman Chemical was experiencing chronic failures to meet internal deadlines. They decided to try a new tactic and *reward* their team for meeting a planned completion date by celebrating what they called Gravy Day, at which company executives would serve biscuits and gravy to the employees on the team. They tracked their progress. The deadline date was December 31. The project was completed by mid-November. (Entrepreneur.com, 2003)

Of course! Our Inner Animal is motivated more quickly when rewards exceed consequences. Who wouldn't get a kick out of having their boss serve *them*, even just for just an hour? Sometimes even a token reward can be enough to motivate or make an employee feel valued. I have been known to reward well-performing employees with everything from a Starbucks card to a weekend for two in Carmel-by-the-Sea. The point is that every employee will be motivated by their own self-interest *more* than the needs of the company. It is the clever and effective manager that comes up with ways to meet their employees' instinctive personal needs while at the same time serving the company's interests.

Of course, including a reward in your assignments is not a guarantee of results. There may indeed be a deeper disturbance in the force, perhaps even some confusion in your department hierarchy. If meeting deadlines is a consistent problem in your office and simple motivation has not been attractive enough to sway your staff, they may not be accepting your legitimacy as the leader. This would be a structural weakness in your *department's* Happy Pyramid!

The solution here would be to first repair the damaged foundation of the Pyramid, specifically Steps 2, 3 and 4: Situational Awareness, Personal Boundaries and Acceptance. Each employee under your direction must acknowledge who has power and where they stand on the status ladder, know the expectations and limits of their own position and accept it all accordingly.

Luckily, Bessy's Fearless Follow-Through helps shore up all three of those Steps! Reminding an employee about the deadline approaching casts you in a leadership position from the get-go. Getting their commitment to meet the deadline by a specific date clarifies their Personal Boundaries and expectations. Once the promised deadline is met, it solidifies their Acceptance of your leader/follower relationship. By the same token, attaching a *consequence* to non-compliance automatically makes *compliance more pleasant* by contrast. Our instinct to choose pleasure over discomfort takes over and makes it easier for the employee to "Accept" the role of follower.

On the other hand, if the employee routinely commits to deadlines but does not meet them, this is an employee that cannot be taken at their word. They have failed the first Step of the Happy Pyramid (Trust), and you may be well-advised to consider letting them go. Without Trust, harmony and a fully productive relationship will never be possible with this employee and their bad example could trigger the instinct to Imitate this disrespect for authority throughout the workplace. I often think of the adage shared with me long ago by one of my respected business mentors: "Hire thoughtfully; fire quickly."

Situation: Absenteeism and High Turnover

No sooner than you've trained a new office manager than he or she quits and you have to start all over again, costing your company valuable time and money. What's more, your key departments are always short-handed due to workers not showing up for one reason or another, causing their coworkers (who never miss work) to take up the slack. Your dependable workers are now on the verge of burnout, feeling understandably resentful. You fear they might leave as well.

Understand It:

If our human instinct is to Seek Pleasure and Avoid Discomfort, when staff do not show up for work or quit prematurely it begs the question: Might there be something uncomfortable at work for these employees?

Some turnover is inevitable in any business, especially in the lower-paid, entry-level jobs. These are not intended to be permanent positions but rather stepping stones to other, more advanced, and higher-paid ones. If your company does not have those advanced positions available, know that your employees needing those higher-earning positions will find advancement elsewhere, and plan for that. But if you see your higher-paid management leaving frequently, their Inner Animal is probably driving them to it. Either the environment is unpleasant, and they seek a more pleasurable one elsewhere (pleasure over discomfort), or the resources they need are more plentiful elsewhere (i.e., more money, benefits, etc.).

In short, people leave companies for all sorts of reasons—the ones they state and the ones they *feel*. Let's dig deeper behind what the departing employee formally states as their reason for leaving and uncover the *possibly deeper* reason . . . the one coming from their Inner Animal.

The reason they're stating:

Frequently, employees who quit a company cite uncaring or unprofessional management as their reason for leaving. Comments might include being overworked and under-appreciated, not being listened to or that the company values speed or profits over quality of work.

The instincts they're feeling:

Every business has certain profits and margins that must be met for financial sustainability, but when management focuses too heavily on numbers *instead of the people that produce them*, problems with employee morale and retention are predictable. Being treated like a number instead of a human being thwarts one of our deepest instincts—the Desire to be Important! A company valuing speed over quality or being dismissive of feelings relating to business decisions can fly in the face of an employee's need to *matter* and can be at the root of many resignations.

It is imperative to state here that *the distance between what a manager wants and what they get is their people.* People are the link and the bridge. If people were machines, management would be simple: Just insert the assignment at one end, crank the handle and retrieve the finished product at the other end. Of course, people aren't machines, yet surprisingly I see many managers with this mechanical approach.

No wonder they are routinely frustrated and "disappointed" in staff that do not live up to expectations. How could they?

Make no mistake, employees will leave when management does not recognize and respect their humanity. Good management is complicated because it requires an acceptance that employees' feelings are *relevant*. A commitment to this managerial acceptance seems imperative in order to receive the most from people. But this can only be done by *understanding* these emotions in the workplace, *predicting* them and, ultimately, *molding them toward compliance*. This is what I mean by "influence through instinct." Granted, this instinct-savvy style of management may seem less efficient than the straight-line "Git'er done" approach, but at the end of the day, a respected and valued staff member will always get the job done faster than a resentful or resistant one.

The reasons they're stating:

Another common reason cited for leaving a company is perceived favoritism in pay or promotions and the resulting perception that opportunities for career growth or advancement are too limited or non-existent.

Understand the instincts they're feeling:

Our instincts understand a pragmatic reality: Those who deserve more get more, etc. When this instinctive belief is violated by other factors such as favoritism, people predictably fight back! Jealously comes to the fore and employees head for the door.

The reasons they're stating:

Excessive workload without necessary training, resources, or tools to complete assignments or meet deadlines is another common reason employees give when leaving a company.

The instincts they're feeling:

When expectations exceed someone's ability to meet them, it confounds their instinctive desire for Group Harmony and Cooperation because they know their shortcomings will become a problem. Their Desire to be Great is also trounced because even though they want to get the job done, they know they may fail because of factors they see as beyond their control. This inner conflict can be frustrating, humiliating and eventually unbearable. The stress of demands too difficult to meet, coupled with failure of management to see the problem and invest in the training or tools necessary, can push anyone to their breaking point. A machine will just blow a fuse. An employee will quit.

Avoid Ritzi-Rude, Scaredy-Cat and Nellie-Nice:

I have friends in a nearby town who run a small appliance store. One manager handles home deliveries and installations while the other manages the sales department, which includes supervising the sales floor and the hiring, training, and scheduling of the salespeople.

The company has struggled with employee turnover in the sales department for years. It's not so much a problem of absenteeism; after a few weeks or months, salespeople just don't show up at all. The sales department manager complains that none of her people follow her directions though she repeats herself and her directives over and over, becoming more frustrated each time. The sales staff works on commissions. One of her senior sales staff routinely pushes his way to walk-ins and the commissions they represent to the detriment of the newer, less bold floor staff. The manager won't confront the bully about this. (Personally, I think she's intimidated by him herself.) From my perspective it's not difficult to see why there are issues in the company with staff retention. The sales manager has chosen a Scaredy-Cat (non-)Action Style, opting to avoid dealing directly with the offending salesperson

Many managers fall prey to the Scaredy-Cat trap. They don't want to offend a key employee or hurt his or her feelings for fear they might leave. The irony is obvious, in that by trying to avoid driving an employee away because of an uncomfortable conversation, they do just that by allowing an intolerable work environment to develop and continue, driving many more employees away over time.

To her credit, my friend is passionate about her business, expressing this passion with her ebullient, demonstrative Nellie-Nice greetings, to the delight of her regular clients whenever they walk into the store. With her customers, she is a Nellie, as they control her income, so this works. As a boss, however, she is in a Bessy position, but where her emotionality can play out in quite another extreme with her staff. When things go wrong (as they inevitably do with her lack of clear leadership), she'll quickly reach a flash point and yell at an underperforming employee, unleashing Ritzi-Rude instead of a calm and focused Bessy-Boss. She wonders why it's so hard to keep employees, but she is Scaredy-Cat, Nellie-Nice, and Ritzi-Rude all rolled into one. Everything *except* the Bessy-Boss she needs to be.

Take Action with Bessy-Down:

Do not depend on loyalty to keep your employees in place. They are human animals with deep-seated needs for predictable leadership, safety, pleasure, group cohesiveness, and resources for survival. Need will trump loyalty most of the time.

If your business is losing employees at a higher rate than you think it should, try looking at your business environment with fresh eyes. Perhaps the problem of employee retention has more to do with their Inner Animal and your management style than you realize. Zip up those emotions, stop trying too hard to be liked, and just put on your Bessy pants! Write out your Bessy-Down Action Plan and get to work. Once you get the hang of it, it's not difficult, though it does take effort.

- Be clear about your expectations.

- Be unafraid to follow through with staff who may not be performing up to expectations.

- Be fair to your employees and treat them with respect, even when disciplining.

- Stay calm and focused like the Leader every employee wants and needs.

If you do these things, chances are the people you have hired and invested in will stick around because you are meeting their deepest needs. Working for you and your company will be more of a pleasure than a chore. (Another instinct met!)

Situation: Rivalry between People or Departments

I own a large dog-boarding and training facility with several interrelated departments and many staff members. Because of the unavoidable human instinct of Rivalry, I know there is an ever-present risk of tension between the kennel department (in charge of the daily care of the clients' dogs), the training department (that trains the dogs according to the owners' wishes), and the main office (which is responsible for all direct communication with the dog owners and funneling pertinent owner requests to both the kennel and the trainers. Any shortcoming in one department will impact the other. A missed nature walk or swim by the kennel means the office has to call the owner and deal with their disappointment firsthand, even though it was not their "fault." Likewise, an inaccurate invoice by the office puts the trainer in an awkward position with the dog owner when it's time to pay the bill at graduation. Incomplete or missing instructions to the kennel by either the trainers or the office can mean the dog's care by the kennel staff is less than promised, though the kennel was not responsible for the miscommunication. The blame game and passing the buck among multiple departments can create an unhealthy "us vs. them" attitude in any business. I'm sure you've seen it in your own workplace or heard about it from your partner or friends.

Understand It:

If you are experiencing Rivalry between people and departments, don't panic. Your company is not full of mean-spirited workers, just workers unconsciously operating on their instincts. The tension of Rivalry you are witnessing has its roots in their Inner Animal layered with their instinct of Competition and the ever-present Desire to be Great or Important. If one department's actions or inactions make everyone in another department look bad, it understandably rubs these instincts the wrong way. Our natural "us vs. them" mentality, and people's loyalty to one's group and distrust of "outsiders" makes managing a multidimensional office environment even more challenging. You could say the workplace is a veritable instinct stew!

Avoid Ritzi-Rude, Scaredy-Cat and Nellie-Nice:

Don't blame, enable, or avoid the Rivalry issue here. Those Ritzi-Rude, Scaredy-Cat and Nellie-Nice techniques probably aren't going to solve this. Bessy-Boss, along with an understanding of instincts, is what is needed to rescue this situation and influence a better outcome.

Take Action with Bessy-Down:

Getting to the root of the problem will be the very best way to solve Rivalry issues. Let me explain by way of something I have done in my own company:

Every week we started having interdepartmental meetings, with the supervisor from each department attending and giving a brief report of current department activities and projects. These inclusive meetings foster familiarity and a greater understanding of the workload and pressures being handled by each department. Right away, coworkers began seeing each other more as individuals than adversaries. Department shortcomings, when they occur, seem a little more understandable within the greater picture and broader awareness.

We also created company projects and assign project teams to carry them out. A project team is made up of individuals from different departments. In essence, we created a new "Group," with loyalties and friendships that cross department lines. The department heads slowly became more familiar with each other as people instead of just names on a company chart.

Finally, striving for a Nellie-Up Action Style of friendship and harmony *between* coworkers, we plan company events and parties throughout the year to get all employees from all departments socializing as friends. Things like movie nights in the office, BBQs for employees and their families and even a float committee for our local parade. All these activities help promote a larger sense of Grouping and cohesiveness. In short, the more friendships thrive in your workplace, the greater the spirit of cooperation will thrive.

Situation: Gossip

You hear through the grapevine that so-and-so on your staff had another weekend binge and might have a secret drinking problem, that the employee out on questionable disability was seen chopping wood yesterday afternoon, and that your most valuable employee might be applying for a job with your competitor. You don't know whether to be angry or grateful for these insights.

Understand It:

Our instincts run deep and Gossip—believe it or not—is one of them. Did you know that gossip has been around since early man? If fact, it was a survival technique! Here is what author, Nigel Nicholson, wrote in the July-August issue of *Harvard Business Review* in his article, "How Hard-Wired is Human Behavior?": (Nicholson, 1998).

> *"Along with scarcity of food, clothing, and shelter and the constant threat of natural disaster, the Stone Age was also characterized by an ever-changing social scene. From one season to the next, it was not easy to predict who would have food to eat, let alone who would be healthy enough to endure the elements. In other words, the individuals who ruled the clan and controlled the resources were always changing. Survivors were savvy enough to anticipate power shift and swiftly adjust for them, as well as those who could manipulate them. They were savvy because they engaged in, and likely showed a skill for gossip. Even in today's office environment, we can observe that expert gossips time and again know key information before everyone else. That has always been true in human society."*

Still today we seem instinctively attuned to every nuance of change in the group dynamic because our survival instincts have never gone away. If human gossip is instinctively driven, managers will never rid their workplace of it entirely. There are, of course, ways to cleverly control and manage it, but eliminate it? Never!

Believe it or not, gossip, per se, may not be a bad thing. In fact, it can serve its original purpose of sounding the early alert to approaching problems or issues in any workplace. As a manager you must, however, take appropriate steps to make sure gossip is kept in reasonable check and is not malicious or damaging.

Avoid Ritzi-Rude, Scaredy-Cat and Nellie-Nice:

Yelling or wagging a Ritzi-Rude finger at gossipers will not stop them. In fact, they'll probably start gossiping about *you!* A manager who ignores a gossip problem at work like a Scaredy-Cat, just hoping it goes away on its own, is foolhardy. Becoming a Nellie-Nice friend with the gossipers might keep you out of their nasty grapevine, but they'll just gossip about others. Bessy-Boss to the rescue!

Take Action with Bessy-Down:

Here is what we do at my kennel, and it has proven invaluable when we must (inevitably) have the "gossip conversation" with an employee. We use this company procedure not only to manage gossip, but all manner of predictable problem behaviors in the workplace.

It starts at the hiring process. As we narrow our hiring search to several candidates, we have a conversation with each about our company values and culture prior to their signing on the dotted line. Our "brand" is verbally summed up in the following way: *We treat every client as a friend and every dog as our own. We treat each other like we would want to be treated ourselves, and the company is dedicated to providing its employees as positive, pleasant, and supportive a workplace as possible.* This begins to solidify Step 3 of our Pyramid, Personal Boundaries, so all job candidates will know early on what we will expect of them as well as the boundaries that will limit their behavior.

When we have a finalist, our conversation gets more detailed as we go over a written document we call our Employee Pledge, which lists in greater detail what we expect from our employees and what they can expect from the company. This further develops Step 3 of our company's Happy Pyramid: Personal Boundaries. We include pledges like promising mutual respect of coworkers, a positive attitude, enthusiastic energy, and a gracious demeanor at all times when at work, as well as promises to refrain from gossip, profanity, disrespectful behavior toward coworkers or insubordinate behaviors toward management. If the prospective new hire is comfortable with this, they *sign* the document for their file and get a copy of their own. This initiates Step 4 on the Pyramid, Acceptance. Then the rest of the formal hiring documents are completed.

Even with this pledge and initial conversation, however, we know that there will likely be the need to call an employee to task when they start coloring outside the lines of their pledge and our company culture. Our Employee Pledge may not have the force of law, but it documents that we have discussed, and the new hire has *agreed* to, specific standards of conduct. Their signature on the document provides a solid foundation for any disciplinary conversation in the future should one be needed, and it is invaluable in keeping the conversations between employee and management pragmatic, professional, and to the point. In other words, it lays the groundwork for Bessy's Fearless Follow-Through!

There's one final note I'd like to mention when it comes to maintaining a pleasant workplace. It has to do with our instinct to Imitate. In my experience, Attitude and company tone come from the *top*. I've yet to know a company with a cranky owner to have a pleasant and magnanimous staff. On the other hand, I have found that warm and friendly company offices usually have a boss that is a walking example of kindness and civility. It just makes sense. You-know-what rolls downhill and staff below are rarely able to rise above it. Believe me, this monkey-see, monkey-do is no coincidence. Bear cubs learn to hunt by imitating their mothers. A puppy learns how to open a cabinet door by watching his older, four-legged brother do it. When it comes to humans, Imitation is a powerful, instinctive force driving our Inner Animal, and cleverly directed, can be a powerful management tool. Left alone or allowed to go in the wrong direction, it can spell ruin for a workplace.

Recognizing the influence of Imitation, a company that wants to avoid internal gossip must hire managers who do not gossip. If managers want their staff to be nice to each other, they must themselves be nice to *their staff*. In fact, I have found that when hiring for our own business, we hire personality over experience. We can change and increase a person's skill level through training, but we can't change a personality. As one of my fellow business owners once confided, "I can't change bitch." How true.

Situation: Office Cliques

A few of the young women in your office socialize regularly outside of work. While friendships are fine, you are now hearing rumors that some of the other staff are being made to feel left out, looked down upon, uncool, or inferior by this group of "Mean Girls." You wonder how to address this now and how to prevent this type of thing in the future. After all, what employees do in their free time is their business, not yours, right?

Understand It:

Because of our Grouping and Similarity Attraction instincts, humans in a workplace will always have an innate desire to group together with individuals that share common interests or characteristics. Trying to "ban" cliques would be as futile as trying to stop a speeding locomotive.

In my dog company operation, we see the more confident dogs playing together, but often driving away or being less accepting of the weaker or nervous dogs. The rough and tumbles stick together while the meek and milds band together separately, each finding comfort in their respective similarities.

There is undoubtedly an element of power and hierarchy in this office clique scenario. Banding together can make people feel more powerful; it's social power. Coauthor of *Mean Girls at Work,* Katherine Crowley, says, "We find that office cliques tend to form in corporate environments with weak management. They are like office gangs that emerge to fill the void of leadership." (Crowley, 2012)

Wow. Many of us will be surprised at that, but voids in leadership are always filled in the Animal World, as a group cannot survive long-term without a hierarchy and a structure. If the animal filling the leader gap is poorly suited for the job, life in the pack or herd may be tumultuous until a more qualified applicant is put in place. Such can be the case with office cliques wielding their power until management steps more effectively into their leadership role.

Avoid Ritzi-Rude, Scaredy-Cat and Nellie-Nice:

A Ritzi-Rude bully won't fill a leader void, since she isn't one. Scaredy-Cat is the furthest thing from a power figure we can think of and Nellie-Nice is a friend, not a superior. You guessed it. This situation calls for Bessy-Boss.

Take Action with Bessy-Down:

I find the analogy between office cliques and street gangs fascinating, in that both can emerge to fill a void in leadership, one within the office and the other possibly in the home. Frequently, managers at work are not aware of weak points in their leadership, but it's actually a pretty common issue, as are cliques, and employees becoming clique members, filling the perceived power gap at work with a hierarchy of their own.

Here's a problem where the solution comes by tweaking the things that may have caused it to happen in the first place: *Instincts and an unstable Pyramid.* In this case, separate sub-groupings have developed within the workplace and with them, the inevitable instinct of Rivalry. This clique has formed because the Situational Awareness and Personal Boundaries Steps, within the Pyramid, might need to be addressed with greater clarity. Here are some ideas:

- Come up with some activities or committees that will "cross-pollinate" your workplace to build on the Grouping instinct through more common interests and less Rivalry.

- Perhaps form a committee of selected individuals to work on a community project together.

- Set up an on-going meeting schedule to assure they are interacting.

- Ask for weekly progress reports. By doing this, you are demonstrating strong leadership while also addressing the root cause of clique.

To feed their Desire to be Great or Important, be sure that when the project is completed, you publicly recognize all the project committee members for a job well done. A photo of the team in the company newsletter might not be a bad idea, either.

Get your Bessy on when it comes to leading your troops. Be strong, be clear, be consistent and unafraid. Avoid Ritzy-Rude and Scaredy-Cat Action Styles. Follow your Bessy's Fearless Follow-Through plan. If things do not improve, talk to the "mean girls" and make sure *they* know that *you* know what's going on and that you are very "disappointed" in their behavior. Mean Girl leaders can have an unusually high Desire to be Important, so expressing disappointment in their behavior might stop the Mean Train in its tracks.

If the hurtful gossiping continues, meet again and explain that the behavior needs to stop immediately and have each commit to that verbally. Send each an email confirming their stated commitment. If they fail to keep their commitment, be prepared to follow up with the appropriate consequences. While we're at it, let's not forget that increased comradery and positive social connections between coworkers and departments along with smart leadership can help inoculate your workplace against cliques in the future.

Are There Staff Situations Not Solved by Bessy-Down Leadership?

The fact is that not all problems or situations are fixable, but this is not a failure of Bessy-Down. When Bessy-Down management fails to produce results, it is nearly always due to deeper problems climbing the Steps of the Happy Pyramid itself. Either the subordinate has refused to Accept his or her role relative to a Bessy (Step 4), or Personal Boundaries are unclear (Step 3), or there is general confusion in Situational Awareness (Step 2) regarding who actally occupies the higher status rung. It could even be a deeper issue involving a basic lack of Trust by one or both parties (Step 1). It all comes back to the Pyramid and its Seven Steps!

Nellie-Up

Using Nellie-Up and Instinct-Savvy with Your Boss

Unlike the previous section, where we explored the tools presented for someone in a position of greater power and status, here we are examining how to get what we want without that benefit. From this "non-boss" position, we can only *influence* rather than demand. To assure your greatest success in currying favor, generosity, and cooperation from your superiors, Nellie-Up should consistently be your Action Style. It's Nature-tested and approved.

A similar Inner Animal lives in your boss, your manager and in you. Understanding basic instincts and how to use them to your advantage can enable you to influence your manager's behavior even without the benefit of status or power.

First, Get in the Right Frame of Mind to Call on Your Inner Nellie

Bringing problems or requests to the attention of your boss is not easy. If you take the wrong approach, you risk a lot. It is in these delicate situations that you'll be best served by a Nellie-Up approach.

First, recognize the instincts that are creating the issues in the first place. Then understand the problem instead of reacting to it. Finally, take a Nellie-Up approach to negotiations for your greatest odds of success in getting what you want while still retaining a positive relationship with your manager. The more consistent you can stay with Nature's model and the Steps of the Happy Pyramid, even without status on your side, the more successful you will be!

Your "Nellie-Up" Guide for the Workplace . . . with Your Boss or Supervisor

- Earn the Trust and admiration of your boss.

- Demonstrate your loyalty and commitment to the company.

- Wait for the right time to ask for anything special.

- Frame your requests in a way that demonstrates how it would also benefit your boss.

- Be willing to graciously take "No" for an answer.

- Be agreeable all the time, with everyone.

- Be a predictable ally.

Situation: Feeling Undervalued or Unappreciated

You are working really hard at your job. You are productive, always punctual and take on more responsibility wherever you can. Yet, your manager doesn't seem to notice. When she does give you an assignment, she hovers over your shoulder to make sure you're doing it right, like she doesn't have faith in your abilities. You haven't had a performance review or a raise in over a year. You wonder if your effort is worth it. Maybe you shouldn't care so much or work so hard if no one appreciates it anyway.

Understand It:

Clearly, your Desire to be Important is not being fulfilled! We all want to be recognized for our good efforts and get feedback that we're on the right track. Without praise and positive reinforcement, the desire to work diminishes rapidly. It's no wonder you're feeling down. To explore this common problem, an organization called the Energy Project partnered with *Harvard Business Review* to find out what most influences people's engagement and productivity at work. The findings showed that employees are vastly more satisfied and productive when four of their core needs are met, one of which included *feeling valued and appreciated for their contribution*. (*Harvard Business Review,* June 18, 2012)

Avoid Bessy-Boss, Ritzi-Rude and Scaredy-Cat:

Forget what you've been told about marching into the boss's office and demanding more respect or appreciation. Unless you work for a Scaredy-Cat that you can bully and intimidate, that type of unfounded Bessy-Boss approach will most likely backfire. It may even get you branded as "insubordinate," which is exactly what you are when you start telling your own superior what you expect *them* to do for *you*. In Nature's world, only a legitimate Bessy-Boss has the right to demand, and you are not Bessy in this relationship. It is important to note, however, there is a world of difference between *demanding* and *confidently requesting*. Only Bessy-Bosses can demand; but everyone else can cleverly request.

Likewise, you must avoid being pouty, resentful, complaining, blaming, or emotional about this while in the workplace. That emotional,

Ritzi-Rude Action Style will not only be ineffective but could likely get you written off and branded as just another "emotional woman," diminishing everything you might bring up in the future. Instinct causes us to "classify" others, and once you've been classified as emotional, reactive, less-than-logical, or worse—hysterical—getting others to see you differently will be difficult. When people say first impressions count, they aren't kidding. Mother Nature invented it. This fact alone should keep you mindful of avoiding emotional extremes in your dealings with your superior.

Of course, if you choose the Scaredy-Cat approach, nothing will ever change or improve because Scaredy-Cats don't have the gumption to do anything about their problems, other than complain about them. Enough said.

Take Action with Nellie-Up:

If you're feeling undervalued or unappreciated, it's time to talk with your boss, but in a friendly, professional manner. You are in the non-boss position here, so Nellie-Up is your best and likely your only strategy for success. You must not demand, insist, or threaten to quit unless you are more appreciated, unless you want to offend your boss's Inner Animal and be shown the door straightaway.

Instead, Give Your Boss a Reason to Value You More Highly:

Set the stage. Before you speak with your manager, do some important groundwork. Earn your boss's admiration so that you rise to the top of his or her mind and earn their Trust. You must first prove that you are a loyal member of the team and committed to the company, not just your own self-interests. Develop Trust and affirm your respect for your manager. Without this critical stage, any request from you might seem too self-serving or presumptive. Here are a few ideas on how to set the stage for future success with your boss or manager:

- Explain how you love your job and the company.

- Express your desire to help the company grow and *their* department to excel.

- Ask your supervisor for feedback on how you are doing and if you might schedule a performance review soon to make sure you're on track with *both* department or company goals.

- Ask if there is a project you can help with. Mention your other skills or talents that may not be known or suggest a project that you would like to take on that could showcase your skills.

Believe me, if one of my staff approached me in this respectful and helpful way, they would rise to the top of my admiration list! Once Trust and admiration are in place, you are in a much better position to have your request granted because of the generosity your boss now feels toward you. As you prepare to talk with them, remember that, like you, he or she also has a Desire to be Great or Important. Keep this in mind as you formulate your talking points. Frame your discussion in a way that positions your request as something that could further your boss's own personal or professional goals. The answer may be "No," but therein lies another important lesson: Be willing to take "No" for an answer, keeping in mind there will be other opportunities for other requests down the line. Personally, I have found that when some doors close, others usually open, and many times these unseen doors reveal an even greater prize. Patience is indeed a virtue, both in life and in careers.

Situation: Low Pay

You think you deserve a raise. Your friends in other companies are getting more per hour than you, for basically the same type of work and responsibilities. Your boss seems to give you a bigger workload than your coworkers, and you wonder if it's because yours is the lowest hourly wage and he or she is taking advantage of you.

Understand It:

No one likes to feel taken advantage of. Again, low pay pokes at our instinctive Desire to be Important and perhaps our Rivalry instinct as well, as we compare our pay to others'. Your feelings are understandable. Your boss, however, also feels the need to do well in his or her superior's eyes. In this situation they are probably evaluated on how well they control payroll costs within the company, and keeping hourly wages under control helps them get favorable performance reviews or even bonuses. Not giving you a raise in a while is likely not personal at all, but more of a pragmatic choice on your boss's part. After all, the boss is being judged on their performance as well. Their instincts of both Loss Aversion and Resource Guarding are powerful motivators to protect their own job and income by keeping payroll expenses in check. Don't feel offended; just make a plan for getting that raise you want, Nellie Style.

Avoid Bessy-Boss, Ritzi-Rude and Scaredy-Cat:

Expecting a raise and demanding your boss give it to you is not a wise plan, as you've not of a current status to justify that type of Bessy-Down approach. What's more, your boss may start to see you as problem instead of an asset. Getting angry and Ritzi-Rude with your boss or implying he is intentionally taking advantage of you by paying you less than you are worth would be equally ill-advised. Ritzi-Rudes are seen as adversaries. Bosses want allies! Who do *you* think they will pay more? My money is on the ally, and so is theirs.

Of course, if you choose a Scaredy-Cat (non-)Action Style, well, you've got no one to blame but yourself for not getting that raise. Scaredy-Cats won't even ask!

Take Action with Nellie-Nice:

Since you are an employee dealing with a boss, Nellie-Up is, of course, your best strategy model. No demands, just friendly influence. Here's a possible discussion outline:

- Politely ask for some time with your boss.

- Open the meeting with an explanation that it's a little uncomfortable, but you'd like to talk about your pay and whether he or she thinks you might deserve a small raise.

- Explain that you are aware pay rates are not about keeping employees happy, and that you know there's an entire equation for a company's profitability where payroll expense plays a big part.

- Explain that since your last raise (or since you were hired), you've taken on more responsibilities (list them) and are more efficient and productive (list examples of what you mean).

- Commit that if given a raise, you would expect to be assigned more tasks so you can "pay your way."

- Express your commitment to the company and its success.

- Ask if your boss would give it some thought and meet with you again a week from now to discuss his or her decision (set a date and time).

This is respectful, professional and to the point. No demands, histrionics, or drama. Any boss would respect this type of request. They may not be *able* to grant the request, but at the next opportunity, I would bet you'd be first in line for that raise.

Situation: Passed Over for a Promotion

You were so excited. A position opened in your company that would mean a promotion for you. You believed that your performance had been impressive and sure that you must have outperformed your peers who might also be applying. In fact, you had so many additional qualifications that you knew you were a shoo-in. *But they selected someone else!* Was your boss crazy? Is there any future for you with this company? You are surprised, frustrated, hurt and disappointed. You feel like quitting—after you give your idiot boss a piece of your mind, of course.

Understand It:

Whoa! Down, girl. Your Desire to be Important just got smashed into a wall, so understand that your emotional reaction is instinctive but may not be justified. Maybe you were *over*-qualified. Or someone else had more experience or was just more suited for the duties of that job.

Avoid Bessy-Boss, Ritzi-Rude and Scaredy-Cat:

Of course, you're not Bessy in this situation so a demand for a selection re-do would be inappropriate. A Scaredy-Cat response would be to simply suffer and stew in silence, solving nothing. An angry, emotional Ritzi-Rude response would be the most tempting, but *don't do it!* Even though you're crushed, take a moment and think outside the box of your own hurt feelings. You don't know the details or the company's full rationale behind their promotion decision. You need to face the cold, hard fact that there could, just *could* have been someone else better qualified than you. Choosing someone else for the position most probably wasn't personal.

Vent your anger over this loss, if you have it, at home and in private but resist the urge to do so at work or with your boss. Ritzi- Rude needs to stay in the closet! She is not your friend and her Action Style will not help you. In fact, Ritzi-Rude behavior can be an enemy to your future with not only the company but in life. Take an honest look at yourself and your go-to Action Style in other disappointing personal situations. Choosing a Ritzi-Rude Action Style could well be holding you back more than you know, and you may be missing out on more than just this promotion.

Take Action with Nellie-Up:

While it's extremely disappointing to be passed over for that promotion, you must try not to take it personally. Cool your jets and look forward to the next opportunity for advancement. Muster all of your self-control and respectfully ask for a time to meet with your boss to find out more about the selection process. Ask for feedback on what you might do to qualify for the next promotion opportunity. You will score points on your professionalism and, more importantly, come away with valuable information to improve your odds of success next time.

The following actually happened to me early in my career. I had just gotten married and followed my husband from California to Nevada, leaving a prestigious job in consumer affairs with the federal government in San Francisco. Once settled, I saw a job posting for a consumer affairs position with a small state government office nearby. I applied, certain that I was so incredibly qualified they would jump at the chance to hire me. They chose someone else. After I picked myself up off the floor, I calmly phoned the director of that department and politely introduced myself. I told him I had been an applicant and understood they had hired someone else. Then I told him I was sorry and (tongue firmly planted in my cheek) that they had made a "big mistake." I think we even laughed together at that. This bold but pleasant phone call, however, must have scored some points because several weeks later that same director called me back and asked if I was still interested in the position! I took it.

My point by sharing this story is this: Instead of choosing to react to this disappointment in an angry, Ritzi-Rude fashion or just giving up and retreating under my desk like a Scaredy-Cat, I somehow mustered up the courage and self-control to call the director who had passed me over and pleasantly explained that I was still interested and available. Using humor in this case by jokingly telling him he'd made a "big mistake" broke the tension and made the conversation so much easier. In fact, it might have been the most important element of the conversation, because through wit and laughter, I came across as a likable and reasonable person. It put me at the top of his list when the position was reopened.

Use Nellie-Up with Your Coworkers . . . and Why

In the case of coworkers over whom you have no formal organizational authority, your only good option is to influence, rather than direct; to request rather than demand. Our Inner Animal and the Inner Animal in others around us recognize only superior or subordinate relationships— a straight-line hierarchy of leaders and followers. Subconsciously and instinctively, we perceive others as either possessing higher status than ourselves or lower status, depending on the critical resources controlled, cultural norms or formal organizational structure.

You may not be your coworker's subordinate on the organizational chart, but you are certainly not their superior, so Bessy-Down is off the table. A coworker's Inner Animal will likely react in a *"You're not the boss of me!"* way if you start telling them what to do or how to do it. Your best choice of influence strategy in this situation is to Nellie-Up and use friendly persuasion.

Situation: Not Fitting In

You've just relocated to a new city and started a new job there in a small company where everyone has worked together for years. You're feeling a little like a party crasher and having a difficult time fitting in. Your job is not the problem; it's your coworkers. It feels like they are shutting you out. You are lonely and a bit sad.

Your "Nellie-Up" Guide for the Workplace . . . with Your Coworkers

- Avoid interoffice conflict.

- Foster friendship and harmony with your coworkers.

- Do not give them "orders."

- Do not insist on or compete for your way.

- Be patient.

- Frame any requests as a "favor" or in a way that describes how it would also be beneficial to them.

- Be willing to take "No" for an answer.

- Be agreeable all the time, with everyone.

- Be a reliable ally.

Understand It:

Nothing feels worse than having your most important animal instinct denied: the need to Group and belong. Every *social* mammal on the planet, if they are to survive, finds a home in a group and that group is their bedrock and their security. Lions have their pride; antelope, horses and cows their herd; dogs their pack and humans their family or group of trusted friends. In this case, however, remember that you are walking into an established group, whose initial *instinct* is to distrust outsiders in order to defend and protect their precious "tribe." It's not personal. As it was for our ancient ancestors, the instinct to preserve and protect the Group is strong and it runs deep. Those in your new office feel the need to protect their Group just as you have a need to belong to it.

Avoid Ritzi-Rude and Scaredy-Cat:

Don't' misinterpret the group's hesitation to welcome you with open arms. Don't take it personally. If you do, you'll be tempted to respond like a Scaredy-Cat by isolating yourself and avoiding your new peers because you feel disliked. In Nature's way, , integration into a group takes time. Be patient. After all, to know you is to love you, right?

Obviously, pouting to your friends or your boss that nobody likes you and developing a resentful chip on your shoulder is not the way, either. Sometimes acting like a victim turns you into one. Prickly Ritzi-types that always seem to have a chip on their shoulder are often avoided intentionally, in an ironic self-fulfilling prophecy.

Take Action with Nellie-Up:

The key to being accepted into any group is being friendly, patient, and easy to get along with—like Nellie-Nice. Follow a Nellie-Up Action Plan of fostering friendship and being a predictable ally. Newcomers that are happy and helpful are more rapidly trusted into a group. That's the way Nature has worked for centuries, and it can work for you, too.

First, study your new group and notice what they have in common. Groups attract and accept others with characteristics similar to their own because of our universal Similarity Attraction instinct. Do the women dress in a certain style? Does the staff seem to watch the same shows, see the same movies, like the same restaurants? Try dressing in a similar way, bring yourself up to speed on those shows and movies so you can be conversant about them. Tap into the Grouping and Similarity Attraction instincts of your new workplace, and above all, be friendly.

Earn trust by laying low at first. (No one trusts a kiss-up or a show-off.) Be sure to show up on time for every meeting and contribute in small ways but otherwise go about your business quietly. By doing this you begin to demonstrate that you will be an ally and an asset to the group. Offer to help when appropriate and volunteer for the jobs no one else wants to do. That's very Nellie!

If you need help from a coworker, ask for their advice rather than a physical effort. By doing this, you'll implicitly show that you respect their time as well as their expertise. When you see a coworker that could use help with something, offer it before you are asked by rolling up your sleeves and pitching in. Say good things about other people and never complain. You will become known as someone with a positive attitude. Positive people are easy to Trust. Friendships also develop in positivity and trust, so a positive attitude will open the door to good connections at work. As time goes on, you will benefit from those connections by getting more of what you want from those that like and trust you.

This should be no surprise, since *Trust is Step #1 of our Pyramid.* This is the magic of a winning Nellie-Up Action Style. Include others and they are more likely to include you. Less obvious is the fact that although you might be the new kid on the block, there may be others in the organization that have been there longer but feel like "outsiders" as well. You'll notice them if you pay attention. Maybe it's the person in shipping who always eats lunch alone. Or the one in accounting who always stands at the edge of the group. Say something nice. Make them feel accepted and connected to a larger group than before—even if it's only larger by one. This selfless act of kindness will do more to prove to the group that you are genuine and trustworthy than anything else you do. It can quickly pave the way for your inclusion into the group.

Situation: Slackers

You and your coworker have been assigned a project by your boss. Together you've set weekly project deadlines and it started out well, but now your coworker is not giving it her all. She spends time on her private email, makes personal phone calls multiple times a day, and takes two-hour lunch breaks. You, on the other hand, are arriving on time every day, putting in your full eight hours without personal distractions, and breaking your neck to get back to your desk after your prescribed one-hour lunch. In short, you're taking up your coworker's slack in order to keep the project on schedule so it can be completed by the deadline. To say you are growing resentful is an understatement. You're about to blow.

Understand It:

You are resentful because your Inner Animal sees your coworker slacking off with no consequence and getting the same respect as you without the same effort. Remember that anything less than effort-based outcome is not acceptable to your Inner Animal, so Jealousy is predictably moving in. As for your slacker coworker, her Inner Animal is wired to choose easy over difficult. As long as slacking remains her easier choice, she will probably continue to do so. That said, she is also wired for other instincts that might be tapped as part of your solution strategy.

Avoid Bessy-Boss, Ritzi-Rude and Scaredy-Cat:

Though it's tempting, do not confront or *demand* to your slacker coworker that she stop taking advantage of you and threaten consequence (like going to the boss) if she does not start pulling her weight. It sounds good on paper, but it probably won't stand up to the reality of raw human nature. You are her coworker, not her supervisor, so there's no hierarchical authority to validate that type of Bessy-Boss directive. Certainly, blowing up in anger and frustration like Ritzi-Rude would

111

be a mistake as well, guaranteed to have repercussions down the line in terms of your relationship and overall Group Harmony. Of course, if you choose to do nothing, in Scaredy-Cat style, the problem will only persist and may get worse.

Take Action with Nellie-Up:

Before you jump to the easy conclusion that your coworker is just a lazy so-and-so, consider that there may be other factors driving her behavior—even other instincts. Workers that show up late, leave early, or otherwise seem disconnected to their responsibilities at the office frequently are facing greater issues in their personal lives outside the workplace. Our time at work is but a small piece of our overall life experience. A view from thirty thousand feet is often the clearest.

A colleague that's not giving her all could be experiencing personal difficulties at home, or there might be larger issues that are affecting her attitude and motivation. You can have a conversation with her, but it needs to be compassionate and friendly based, like a Nellie-Nice. Maybe something like, "I can't help but notice you're not as excited about our project as you were at first. Is there anything I can do to help? I'm here if you would like to talk about it." This gets to the matter but in a non-accusatory, non-threatening way. By tapping into your coworker's need to Trust, she might let you inside to the real root of the issue. You could be surprised by what you discover, and it may point the way to a solution.

You might also feed your colleague's Desire to be Great by complimenting her on the admirable sections of the project that she has completed. Mention casually to others in the office (within her earshot) how creative she has been on the project or how careful and thorough on the parts she has completed, etc. Personal success is a funny thing; the more you feel it, the more you believe you are capable of it and the more you want it. It seems that the Desire to be Great often leads us forward.

Of course, your supervisor or manager needs to be aware of what's going on, so respectfully letting them know about the matter is a good idea, but only if it is done in strictest confidence and presented out of concern for the company. The slacker is, in fact, "stealing" time from the organization if they are being paid for not working or doing their personal business on the company clock. Nothing in your relationship with your slacking coworker should change from the positive, however. It's properly in management's hands and with any luck, they're a Bessy-Boss.

Situation: A Coworker Doesn't Seem to Like You

Your boss's administrative assistant is hard to figure out. You have never been unkind to him or done anything to offend him, but he just doesn't seem to like you. He gives you only one- or two-word responses, is rarely pleasant and is generally what you would call unfriendly. You're confused, frustrated and a little hurt. The worst part is, he controls access to your boss. You're never sure he will give him your message or pass along your question.

Understand It:

Keep in mind when interpreting someone's behavior toward you, it's not always about you. People have different personality types and many ways of expressing them. This type of "unfriendly" person might be living behind a crusty shell to protect an inner fragility. In this situation, the administrative assistant could simply be on the far end of the Shyness and Sociability scale. Until they Trust, shy people keep their distance and are quite often misinterpreted or "classified" as cold or unfriendly. The one thing this employee knows is that the boss trusts him to protect his time. With that being the case, he is most likely trying to do right by the boss, not wrong by you. It's not personal.

113

Avoid Ritzi-Rude:

Since it's not personal, don't take this personally. Don't complain to your coworkers about this assistant or join the I-Hate-So-and-So Club with others. Even casual comments about someone's perceived personality flaws can be devastatingly unfair. Your comments will, without a doubt, get back to the assistant, destroying his Trust in you and others and exacerbating the problem. He can't be friendly with people he does not Trust.

While I'm on the subject of talking "confidentially," it's important to know that there is no such thing as a truly confidential working environment within departments! Whether spoken in person, in private text messages, or "in code," information shared with coworkers is *never* private, and for some reason, "bad" information is always leaked the fastest. As my mother used to say, "If you don't have something nice to say about someone, don't say anything at all." If someone at work doesn't seem to like you, don't talk about them. Instead, make it your mission to win them over.

Take Action with Nellie-Up:

Melt the ice and turn a foe into a friend by being Nellie-Nice! A close management colleague of mine had a related experience with an admin assistant notorious for being difficult. None of the other managers wanted her assigned to them. My friend decided to try a different tack. She could see the admin's insecurities and lack of motivation, so she Nellie-Nice'd the heck out of her. Instead of being critical, she treated her kindly, complimented her work, and patiently helped her develop some missing skills. Lo and behold, this prickly staffer blossomed like a cactus flower into one of the company's most admired and prized employees! She became my colleague's most loyal and productive ally, working with her for years. All it took was a deeper understanding and the right Action Style to change the situation and resolve the problem.

I have also been on the receiving end of negative or disagreeable people in my own business. I sometimes come face-to-face with icy scrutiny when I try to convince a potential client to buy the service I'm selling and part with a good sum of money to do so. If they don't seem to like me, instead of retreating to lick my wounds, I remember my favorite axiom about success in sales and in life: *Like Me, Trust Me, Pay Me.* First a colleague or customer must *like you.* Then they are willing to *trust you,* and only then will they *pay you* or grant you what you desire.

If I'm patient and focus on finding something *complimentary* to say about the prospective but unwilling client (like: *"Cool shoes," "Smart question,"* etc.), I can see them slowly start to like me. When I point out things we have in common (like: *"I agree," "You're right about that,"* or *"Oh, I had that happen to me, too!"* etc.), demonstrating that I hear them, sincerely want to help and I'm not just after their money—they begin to Trust me.

In fact, some of my most difficult and initially unfriendly customers have become some of my biggest fans and public advocates—all because I didn't react to their initial negativity personally and patiently employed a Nellie-Up strategy to win them over. Go ahead and try being Nellie-Nice to that admin that seems to dislike you. Let him know you admire his professionalism and that the boss is lucky to have him watching his back. If he has a photo of a teenage son or daughter on his desk, commiserate about how challenging it is to raise a teenager these days, or quietly drop off cookies on his birthday. Do all these things in the spirit of simple friendship, asking nothing in return. If you do this and avoid the pitfalls mentioned above, I promise you can be amazed at what happens. If you are likable and trustworthy, you can overcome his Distrust of Strangers and stimulate his Grouping instinct. His instinctive desire for Group Harmony and Cooperation can do the rest.

Situation: Bullies

You've moved into a new department and need to learn some new skills. An experienced senior member of that department has been assigned to be your trainer. Unfortunately, she doesn't seem to have any patience with you and makes you feel stupid when you don't catch on as quickly as she expects. She even criticizes you in front of your coworkers and in front of clients, leaving you feeling humiliated. You are starting to dread coming to work. You are being bullied.

Understand It:

Believe it or not, the bully in an office is *often* a senior staff member, but it is not as surprising as it seems when you consider all the instincts that are playing out beneath the surface. A newcomer onto her stage could certainly be triggering her natural Distrust of Strangers. If you are smart and talented, there could be Jealousy and Resource Guarding going on, especially if she sees you as someone who could outshine her or even possibly take her job. Her survival instincts could be on high alert and compelling her to drive you away. She may not understand why she's acting the way she is, or even realize she is doing it. It's important for you to be aware of this and know that the bullying isn't about you; it's about *her.*

Avoid Bessy-Boss, Ritzi-Rude and Scaredy-Cat:

Standing up to a bully and demanding that they stop, despite what you have read, is the wrong approach. "Demanding," even quietly, is the purview of the boss only, as making demands requires legitimate higher status. If you are a coworker or a subordinate to the bully, you're not their boss. You do not have *higher* status, so attempts to Bessy-Down on your bully will likely backfire on you. You'll probably seem like an entitled snowflake, making your relationship with the bully even more contentious going forward.

Blowing up in the bully's face in Ritzi-Rude fashion can also fail to solve your dilemma. Ritzi-Rude actions enflame conflict, they do not solve it. Ignoring the bully like a Scaredy-Cat could possibly reduce the voracity of the bullying over time (when the bully finally figures out that her behavior has not gotten rid of you), but do you really want to endure this mistreatment indefinitely?

Take Action with Nellie-Up:

First, let your boss know what's going on, in confidence. Then get on with your Nellie-Up Action plan.

Only Nellie is the real anti-bully. A Nellie-Up Action Plan can see through the smokescreen of bullying behavior and go straight to the instincts driving your coworker's behavior: insecurities about her own status and the need to overcompensate forcefully to keep or elevate her current standing.

The sad fact is the bully is probably not convinced of her own worth, so help assure her. Nellie would *affirm* another's higher status over her own in terms of knowledge and experience (the Acceptance block of our Pyramid). Compliment the bully's skills that you are just now learning from her. If your compliments are overheard by others, even better. Ask how long it took her to get so good at what she does and assume the role of respectful student, grateful for her tutelage. Think *Karate Kid*, with you cast as Grasshopper to her Master. Even if your coworker's initial reception is cool, you can warm her and eliminate her need to bully by building her self-esteem and feeding her Desire to be Great or Important. You can earn her Trust by making your own instinct of Competition seem less of a threat to her. You may not end up best friends, but you can certainly have a peaceful détente, which is a Nellie's secret of success.

Situation: Gossipers and Troublemakers

Your coworker at the desk next to you is always talking about people, and never in a nice way. It's distracting you from your work and making you uncomfortable. After all, your mother always quoted Eleanor Roosevelt, "Great minds discuss ideas; average minds discuss events; small minds discuss people." You don't want to be thrown in with the "small minds," but your coworker just keeps blabbing on. When you don't respond and chime in, she seems to take offense to your silence. You fear your cold shoulder will rub her the wrong way and she'll start talking about *you*.

Understand It:

Don't blame your coworker for being petty or rude. Gossip is primal behavior, and like all our other subliminal drives, it is ultimately related to survival. It was important for early man to know what was going on behind the scenes; to be the first to know information, and to pass it along to the group to avoid impending danger. Today nations have spies, informants and wiretaps to gather developing or secret information. You and I have the internet. Your gossipy neighbor would have been very valuable in the Stone Age, but today she's just disruptive and potentially destructive to the office environment. Bad juju, but fixable.

Avoid Bessy-Boss, Ritzi-Rude and Scaredy-Cat:

If you truly want to stop your coworker's constant gossiping, you must tread very carefully. If you are too Bessy-Bossy, telling her to knock it off *or else*, she'll take offense at what she considers your uppity, holier-than-thou attitude. After all, you're not the boss of her. If you get Ritzi-Rude angry or hurl a personal insult her way in a weak moment, you could start WWIII. You might be tempted to default to Scaredy-Cat, politely nodding along instead of addressing the issue; but if you avoid the uncomfortable conversation, you'll have to live with the uncomfortable office vibe that her gossiping creates.

Take Action with Nellie-Up:

Here's a possible Nellie-Up strategy: The next time your gossiper starts to dish on someone, you can say something in an apologetic tone like, "Wow, that's really interesting, but I'm so sorry—I'm just not comfortable talking about people. Would you mind if we changed the subject?" Or, counter her negative comment with a positive one about the person she's trashing, like, "But I really admire how she parents her kids. She's done a wonderful job with them." Or, my personal favorite, "You know, I wonder if there's not another side to the story? Let's not jump to conclusions. We may owe her that."

By adopting a Nellie-Up Action Style, you will appear the bigger person without shoving it in the gossiper's face or humiliating her by calling her out on her bad behavior. She'll get the point and with any luck, she may even start to Imitate your good manners, substituting an undesirable instinct for a better one.

Situation: Saboteurs and Backstabbers

You've always had a great relationship with your coworkers. Lately, though, you're getting the cold shoulder from some of them and they stop talking whenever you walk into the room. You find out one of your peers and supposedly good friend has shared with the team a confidence—that you are seeing a therapist on a regular basis. Besides feeling betrayed, you worry that this will filter to your boss and might affect your chances for advancement in the company.

Understand It:

Saboteurs and backstabbers have been around since animals themselves. The wily coyote, in particular, has been a master of sabotage, pretending to be playful and innocent to draw in his unsuspecting victim while the rest of his bloodthirsty pack hide in the trees, waiting to descend and feast.

When the human animal, on the other hand, uses sabotage or backstabbing it is much subtler and more civilized. Humans might use it to satisfy, in a twisted way, their instinct to Compete. Instead of working to raise their own situational status through hard work and honest effort, some choose to destroy or socially demote their competitors and gain status by default.

Avoid Bessy-Boss, Ritzi-Rude and Scaredy-Cat:

Since the saboteur in this case is a coworker and not a subordinate, being bossy, rude, or confrontational won't be your route to a solution, though you'll be tempted to react that way when the Judas is exposed. Instead, count to ten and choose a Nellie-Up Action Plan to help solve the problem, even if you'd rather be Scaredy-Cat and hide in a haystack.

Take Action with Nellie-Up:

WWND? *What would Nellie do?* In a situation where outright lies are being circulated about you, a Nellie-Up strategy might be, in fact, to do nothing—not because you want to avoid the issue, but to *prove the saboteur's lies wrong by living the truth.* I have been the victim of lies and sabotage by competitors for many years, but choose to keep going forward undeterred, instead of reacting or even responding. My business keeps growing, while those competitors' businesses do not, thus exposing their lies in a sort of poetic justice. Yes, karma is real.

Ignore the sticks and stones of one and make a point to be a friend to all. Be the consummate professional to your boss. The truth will come out. Your backstabbing "friend" will end up looking foolish and be defanged when others begin to consider the source the next time she tries to plant a destructive rumor. If it makes you feel better, privately remember the immortal words of Marilyn Monroe, "Sweetie, if you're going to be two-faced, at least make one of them pretty." Makes me laugh every time!

So you're on the path to greater success and more productive relationships at work. Brava! Don't forget to add this to your Gratitude list each morning, whether it is a mental list or one that you write down. Even if the progress is slow or incremental, make a point of recognizing the progress and be truly grateful for it. Hopefully, your Attitude about life at work will also start to improve and this shift to positivity in Attitude as well as your growing list of Gratitudes can begin lifting the clouds from this corner of your universe and letting your life sunshine in.

CHAPTER EIGHT

SEVEN EFFECTIVE MAMA DOG METHODS TO MANAGE YOUR KIDS

What mom has not struggled with managing her kids from time to time as they grow, challenge, and test their independence as well as her authority? Raising responsible, kind, thoughtful and well-mannered children is every mother's goal, but some find the road to that goal rockier than others. Regardless of the obstacles life throws you or your kids along your parenting path (bad friends, defiance, disrespect), here are some simple and effective parenting tips from the most experienced and successful mother of all time: *Mother Nature!*

From Mother Nature's perspective, you are clearly in a legitimate position of power with your minor or dependent children. You are the parent. You control their resources, including food and shelter. That spells status, which clearly means you can use Bessy-Down strategies with your kids, along with your new awareness of the instincts that make your kids tick in order to get what you want and need from them.

With your new understanding of the Happy Pyramid, human instincts, and the role they play in your child's behavior, you are now a parent ready to address any kid problem!

Your Bessy-Down Action Guide with Your Kids

- Be a living example for your kids.

- Communicate your rules and expectations clearly.

- Enforce rules consistently, without anger or apology.

- Don't be drawn off-track; stay on message and the matter at hand.

- Don't yell or over-react when rules are broken or behavior is unacceptable.

- Don't be afraid to enforce consequences for broken rules.

- Always pair consequences with an explanation of why they are being applied.

- Always end a consequence conversation with an affirmation of your love and belief in them to do better.

- Be the boss, but be nice about it, acting always with dignity and love.

Situation: Arguing and Talking Back

Your kids talk back rudely when you ask them to do their chores or to stop watching TV. You have let them know that this rude behavior is unacceptable, so you are shocked at their continued disrespect and embarrassed when others hear how your children talk to you.

Understand It:

What parent hasn't struggled with their kids talking back and arguing when they don't agree with something? Odds are they are not being intentionally disrespectful but instead are being driven by their inner instincts. Remember the Happy Pyramid? Your family is its own, separate social group with its own need for social harmony 24/7, so the Pyramid is even more relevant at home than it is at work with your coworkers.

The Pyramid is built on a series of foundational questions requiring answers, including "Who can be trusted?" "Who makes the rules?" and "What is expected of me?" These are likely the questions your children are begging to have answered in their own attempt to climb the Pyramid and find happiness within their family! *Testing behaviors are the acting out of these questions.* Unless the parent can answer correctly and adequately, assuring their children that the foundation of their Pyramid is firmly in place and safe to climb, the path to Happy may be blocked.

Don't think for a moment, however, that once you have answered your child's questions about who makes the rules, they will consistently Accept those rules. We humans, along with every other social mammal, are hardwired to periodically "test" the foundation of Pyramid to be sure it is still structurally sound. We rephrase our questions to the leader through new and sometimes more challenging behaviors, just to be sure the one at the top still has what it takes to effectively serve in that position. Think about this: As a country, the U.S. has elections every four years to affirm its leadership. In families, however, children test the leadership daily. Routine challenge is a constant part of the group dynamic, and an *instinct* in every social mammal. You could safely say a parent is constantly running for reelection!

The main thing to remember when your "little animal" talks back or challenges your authority, it's not personal. See it as their built-in *system test* to affirm your leadership abilities and set their minds at ease.

Avoid Ritzi-Rude, Scaredy-Cat and Nellie-Nice:

Above all, don't be Ritzi-Rude and lose your cool in the face of inevitable kid challenges. If you yell, you've lost before you've begun. Your children need to know that you're strong enough to *control* your emotions. That's the stable leader your little animals can respect and follow. If you take a Nellie-Nice approach, thinking the answer is backing off and being more a friend than a parent, the leader position will be left vacant and the Pyramid shaky. If you decide to do nothing and just let things work out on their own, you've chosen a Scaredy-Cat Action Style and your child's Inner Animal will *still* want to know, "Who's driving the bus and what's my seat assignment?" I've seen these universal questions acted out by dogs many times. Left unanswered, they become "louder" over time with ever-stronger testing behaviors. Both the Nellie-Nice mom and the Scaredy-Cat mom leave the driver's seat empty. No wonder it's such a bumpy ride, regardless of species!

Take Action with Bessy-Down and Influence through Instinct

With your kids, my advice is to be Bessy-Boss and channel her Bessy-Down Action Style. Keeping your cool is the cornerstone of Bessy-Down management and proves you can be in total control in any situation. That's a good start. Being clear about your rules and expectations plus being consistently willing to enforce them with loving fairness completes the picture.

We've all heard about the importance of being consistent. Think about this in terms of the questions your kids are asking when they are argumentative. (Yes, arguing is a question!) Do you address the argumentative behavior as unacceptable sometimes but let it go at other times because you just don't have the energy to deal with it? Remember, the questions being acted out are often, "Who really makes the rules here and what are my boundaries?" Answers to questions must always be consistent, *or they're not answers at all.*

Consider what I call Slot Machine Psychology. We play the slots with the question, "Will I win?" Most of the time, slot machines say "No," take your money and don't pay out. Just as you start to get discouraged, thinking that your behavior will never be successful, your machine hits, the bells and whistles go off and you're a winner. Yes, you *can* win! So, you keep playing, asking the same "Will I win?" question but now *ignoring* the "Nos" because you have been encouraged and even emboldened by the occasional (and you believe the eventual) "Yes."

Casinos have built their fortunes on this principle of intermittent reinforcement, and your kids may be living by it as well. If slot machines or gambling *never* paid, no one would play and casinos and gambling behavior would disappear quickly. Lack of consistency, however, with intermittent reward is gambling's bread and butter because it drives the continuation of gambling behavior.

With your kids, lack of consistency in enforcing your rules and boundaries can also drive them to continue those unwanted behaviors. Times when you "let it slide" could be like hitting that occasional jackpot and not only encourage the bad behavior to continue: It can actually embolden your children to keep at it even when disciplined, if they believe they'll eventually be successful. The answer to stopping a behavior lies in it being *consistently unsuccessful.* If you want a behavior to stop, one way is to consistently stop letting it pay off. Being quietly consistent with your rules can eliminate the reason for your kids to "gamble" with your response.

In our gambling analogy keep in mind the real motivator was the *jackpot reward.* Just as good animal trainers use the power of positive reinforcement to encourage desired alternative behaviors and more willing cooperation along a new path, whenever your *child* cooperates, recognize and reward it! Your praise for cooperative behavior can feed their Desire to be Great. In fact, if this instinct is being starved, talking back and arguing could simply be a plea for recognition. Make sure you look for special talents or abilities that you can encourage and develop in each child. If clear rules, consistent reinforcement and praise for good behavior does not do the trick, try Bessy's Fearless Follow-Through.

For example, if you asked your teenage daughter yesterday to pick up her dirty clothes and put them in the hamper, but she retorted with a snotty comment and the clothes are still strewn across her bedroom floor today, follow through like Bessy. Here is a sample script:

You: *I see your clothes are still on the floor. I'm doing the laundry tomorrow.* (Subtle reminder)

The next morning:

You: *Keep in mind it's your job to get your clothes into the hamper. I'd hate for them to miss the laundry.* (Stronger warning with consequence for non-compliance being clarified.)

That afternoon:

You: *It's unfortunate you missed the laundry. Oh, did you want to wear those jeans to the party tonight? I guess you'll have to wear them dirty.* (Fearless Follow-Through with calm emotion.)

The next time you walk by your daughter's room and it's cleaner, tell her how nice it looks, acknowledge the effort it takes to keep it that way, and let her know how proud you are of her.

To summarize, you have clarified your family Hierarchy and strengthened the foundation of your Happy Pyramid by choosing the Bessy-Down Action Style, setting clear boundaries and enforcing them with strength and kindness. When her behavior begins to improve, you can key into your daughter's instinct to be Great by acknowledging how great she is becoming with her new behavior.

Situation: Defiance

Your child is outright refusing to do what you say and talks back, right to your face. Profanity flies and you are so taken aback, you feel paralyzed and powerless. You're trying to keep your cool but you're feeling drawn into battle.

Understand It:

As happens so often, the problem we think we have may not be the real problem at all. In the case of a defiant child, once again it may actually be a matter of insufficient leadership and the defiance a symptom of it. Let me explain.

In my training school, a defiant dog is usually one that has been without clear leadership long enough to now assume *he* is truly the one in charge. The dog owner has no idea that their leadership has been lacking, so the defiance is shocking to him or her. The owner thought love would be enough to produce a grateful and respectful dog. It's not. I know that Nature's leadership requires more than love. From many years of experience, my assessment is that in addition to a hearty helping of love, the recipe for effective leadership requires hierarchy, rules, and follow-through.

Kids do not seem much different than dogs when it comes to needing Nature's brand of leadership. Mother dogs are not shy about setting and enforcing rules with their pups. They are clearly in charge and just as willing to stop an unwanted behavior as they are to play and love on their young ones. They love freely yet control without apology. They are clearly "driving the bus" and their pups know their seat assignments.

Within your family hierarchy, someone has to drive the bus as well. If parents do not drive, kids probably will. The problem is when kids find themselves in the driver's seat by default, they are ill-equipped to handle the actual responsibilities of the job. They don't know *how* to drive! They've gotten a driver's license without passing the test; and like humans promoted above their pay grade without the necessary skills who turn autocratic with their staff, children can turn to defiance, bullying, and aggression to manage their world. They lack the adult self-confidence required to lead or live with quiet strength. Or, in the case of young people that have been driving their own bus for an extended period, they may actually believe that they *are* the legitimate driver, so when a parent steps in to finally take the wheel, the child *consequences* the parent by being defiant for this seeming "insubordination."

Avoid Ritzi-Rude, Nellie-Nice and Scaredy-Cat:

Take a breath. Resist the temptation to react in angry Ritzi-Rude fashion, even though you may be steaming inside. To give in to Ritzi-Rude and react emotionally to such egregious behavior would most certainly spell defeat.

You may also fail the challenge if you try to be a friend instead of a parent. That type of Nellie-Up strategy is best for subordinates, not for leaders. Ironically, Ritzi-Rude and Nellie-Nice with their lack of follow-through and leadership often embolden children to the point that the parent becomes intimidated. When that happens, the parent retreats to the Scaredy-Cat Action Style and the inmates can run the prison.

Take Action with Bessy-Down and Influence through Instinct:

For any animal that truly believes he is the Top Dog, including a defiant child, one must tread lightly to change the dynamic. Direct confrontation can be a recipe for disaster and heightened aggression. Calm finesse is the way to proceed with defiant dogs, and with your two-legged animals as well. In fact, in my dog training business the more defiant the dog, the quieter and more subtle our training style.

Try this Bessy-Down approach to get your defiant child to come around to your way of thinking with minimum argument and friction.

Instead of focusing on what the child is doing wrong, try praising and rewarding anything they're doing *right*. Play to their ego and pride (their Desire to be Great or Important), an instinct that may have been starved if you have focused mainly on the bad behaviors. If a child is repeatedly and exclusively told they are wrong, eventually they may see no point in trying to be right. When we let a defiant child feel *appreciated* when he or she does certain things (the things you want), the child may become more willing to do these things for you and the defiance will begin to melt away. Every social mammal has an instinctive desire to be appreciated (to be Great or Important) and to get along (in Group Harmony and Cooperation). You may have to dig to find it sometimes, but even telling your child you believe in him or her and backing off from micromanaging for a while can feed this instinct.

Here's something that worked for me as a teenager when I was entering that defiant and rebellious stage. My parents stopped micromanaging and let me make some of my own choices, as long as I accepted the results, whether good or bad.

I remember one night I foolishly let it slip that I'd be out late because my friends and I planned to cruise Main Street. (Yeah, we did that in those days, and it was deliciously fun as we tailed all the cutest boys in the hottest cars and hoped they would park next to us at the bowling alley!)

Dad's eyebrows raised but what came out of his mouth was not what I expected. Instead of putting his foot down and sternly forbidding me to engage in such loose behavior, he said, *"Camilla, I'm not going to forbid you to go tonight. I'm going to leave that decision up to you. I know you'll make the right choice."* Checkmate. Brilliant parenting. By trusting me with the freedom to make my own decision and knowing his lifetime foundation of teaching me that I alone would face the consequences of my actions, my father now showed me that he considered me *capable* of making responsible choices on my own. Because of that respect, I did not want to let him down or throw away my chance to prove I was no longer a child. I didn't go.

If your teen is being defiant, try feeding his or her Desire to Be Great or Important. Recognize the good things and compliment freely. Praise and reward your teen for anything that resembles compliance with your house rules and boundaries. Try trusting by giving him or her some responsibility. Refuse to argue, acknowledge feelings, and *always* let your love show. Your teen may turn away, but he or she hears you loud and clear. Consider this a long-term project and be patiently consistent. Like all of us, your child is influenced at the deepest level by his or her instincts. *Encourage those beneficial instincts and refuse to feed the destructive ones.*

Situation: Direct Disobedience

You ask your child to stop doing something and they do it anyway—or do the exact opposite. You've played the parent card, it did not work and now you're out of options and on the ropes. You're insulted, hurt, and ticked off.

Understand It:

Kids intentionally disobeying parents is an escalated version of testing the leader. Although it takes time to get to this point, direct disobedience can be a clear indication that the parent has unintentionally but consistently fallen short when responding to the tests of leadership. Despite their well-meaning actions and their best efforts to turn their beloved child's behavior around, many parents miss the bull's-eye. This is probably because, from the Inner Animal's perspective, *status is determined by the degree to which one can control or stop unwanted behaviors in others.* By failing to stop disrespectful behavior over time, a parent loses credibility and in the process, their status and authority.

Without a parent earning legitimate and believable status by successfully stopping unwanted behaviors, Step 2 of our Pyramid (Situational Awareness) is in turmoil. From the child's perspective, if their behaviors are allowed to continue unchecked, it translates to status advantage! Having status advantage means *they make* the rules; they don't necessarily follow them. This can be the crux of a disobedience issue. It is a universal truth that when there is a void in leadership, others will rise to fill that void. In this case, it is the child. Nature will not abide a vacuum.

Avoid Ritzi-Rude, Nellie-Nice and Scaredy-Cat:

Many parents faced with a defiant child try all three of these ineffective Action Styles! They try getting angry and punitive like Ritzi-Rude, which can just pour gasoline on an already fiery relationship. They try being a friend, like Nellie-Nice, so as not to poke the dragon their child has become, but there is no leadership in Nellie and this can simply underscore the parents' subordinate role. Sometimes it is all too much for the parent to face, and they simply give up, like Scaredy-Cat, but ignoring a problem doesn't fix it.

Take Action with Bessy-Down and Influence through Instinct:

Your best approach, of course, is to follow your Bessy-Down Strategy, staying calm and focused and making sure you have done your homework. You explain clearly your rules and expectations to your child, as well as the related rewards for cooperation and consequences for resistance. These are not threats; they are measured, reasoned, pragmatic statements of fact, all delivered in a calm and caring manner. Remember that Bessy is cool, focused, and principled. She is unapologetic but also fair, friendly and beloved.

If you've done everything above and the disobedience continues, the most important thing here is to follow through with your appropriate and pre-established consequences, but without criticism or anger.

A simple, well-designed consequence can discourage future disobedience in your kids, while anger or criticism might only make them blame someone or something else, rationalize their behavior, and bruise their ego. For example, if your child knows that if he crosses the highway on a bicycle despite your express rule not to do so, it means he loses not only his bicycle privileges for a week, but video games as well. So, take the privileges away for a week! Not five days. Not next time. But keep it pragmatic without argument or apology. It's either Option A or Option B, and what has been prescribed in either case. Keep it clear-cut and simple. Stay loving and compassionate in your delivery. Like Bessy.

Consequence, by contrast, is an educational tool. It is intended to elicit thought, introspection, and produce a positive change in future behaviors. Consequence must be uncomfortable, yet never frightening or over-the-top. It is commensurate with the offense. Consequence says, "You had a choice between Option A with its reward and Option B with its consequence. You chose B and the consequence. It will not be pleasant for you, but I have faith that you can do better and avoid this in the future."

A leader enforces rules. As we've said, when it comes to status, it's all about who enforces *limits and boundaries.* Making rules is one thing; enforcing them is what matters. If you don't enforce the rules you make, you are not really the leader. Plain and simple. If you are not *being* the leader, your child has no *instinctive* reason to obey you. In fact, instinctively speaking, if you do not set and enforce limits and boundaries, you would for all practical purposes be *subordinate* to your child. In that case, obedience to you would be contrary to your child's instincts! I can hear all you permissive parents groaning now, but this *is* how animals work, and your little animals are probably no exception.

A Word about Consequences

I find that many people confuse consequence with punishment. People often use them interchangeably as terms, but they are not the same! In fact, the nuanced difference between the two is crucial to understand if consequence is to be successfully used in Bessy-Down leadership.

Punishment is payback. It is often emotionally charged and vindictive. Punishment is frequently a form of venting one's anger and is overreactive. Punishment says, "I am furious with you for doing that and I'll make you pay!"

Consequence is none of those things. It is simply the result of an undesired behavior which is less pleasant than the desired alternative. No judgement or finger-wagging. In other words, Option A, this happens; Option B, that happens. You choose.

Situation: Having to Repeat Yourself

You find yourself nagging, "If I've told you once, I've told you a thousand times . . ." or, "How many times do I have to tell you?" You are frustrated and wonder if this behavior is more than just not listening. You're beginning to think your child might be acting passive-aggressively in her disregard toward you.

Understand It:

Having to repeat yourself when it comes to asking your child to do something could simply be a direct result of fuzzy rules and non-enforcement. It's not that your child is not listening. She hears you fine. She either does not know the response you expect (fuzzy rules) or she's figured out it doesn't matter if she ignores you (there's no consequence). This goes directly to Tier 3 of our Pyramid, Personal Boundaries, where the rules and expectations of one's position are laid out and fully explained. *Your child cannot live up to your expectations if they have to guess what they are.*

Then there is that matter of consequences. While we are defining expectations on our Personal Boundaries Tier, we need to also specify consequences for falling short. When all is made clear in Tier 3, there are no surprises going forward. The child who reaches Tier 4, Acceptance, does so knowing the rules of the game and now agrees to play by them. Clear rules and Acceptance of them by both parties are always the best way to avoid conflict, in business and in the home.

Avoid Ritzi-Rude and Nellie-Nice:

It seems obvious, but my advice is to *stop* repeating yourself! Saying things again in a more stern or angry tone, like Ritzi-Rude, won't help. Saying it again nicely, like Nellie, just communicates that your requests come in repetitions of two, three, or four and are not complete until the full range of requests have been expressed. If you have made it clear that you will only say things once, say things *once*.

Take Action with Bessy-Down:

I remember when I was quite young, my mother and I had been invited to come visit a friend in town who had kids my age whom I knew and liked. When it was time to leave, I heard my mom calling me to the car, but I ignored her because I was busy doing something fun. *She left without me.* I was devastated because I missed my opportunity to see my friends and found myself stuck on the farm alone. That was my consequence. From then on, my mom rarely had to repeat herself. I knew what was expected of me and that she was fearless enough to follow through.

Situation: Not Listening

You're talking to your child, but he keeps texting. You ask him to do something, but he remains focused on the computer or the TV. When you ask him about it later, he doesn't remember the conversation or what you asked him to get done.

Understand It:

Our Inner Animal will always honor and respect those of legitimized higher status. By now you probably can predict what I'm about to say. A child that literally does not listen to you is demonstrating a lack of *respect* for you. But don't panic or be offended.

This disrespectful behavior can have underlying causes much deeper than the behavior you are witnessing. As we've seen in so many of these examples, respect is born of rules, follow-through, and quiet leadership. I know it can be difficult for a parent to remember these points and even harder to muster the effort to put them into action every day; yet without rules, follow-through and leadership, children can predictably act out disrespect. Ignoring their parent's words is one of the most common ways.

Avoid Ritzi-Rude, Nellie-Nice and Scaredy-Cat:

Don't get mad, don't repeat yourself, and don't let it go. Get your Bessy on.

Take Action with Bessy-Down:

To change the big picture, earn your child's respect by being his or her Bessy.

As a Bessy, your job is to be a teacher, limit-setter, and life coach . . . not just a friend. Be specific on what is and what is not acceptable behavior.

Don't ignore disrespectful behavior. Step in and call it when it happens. Stay pragmatic but make it clear when your child has stepped outside the set limits. Apply appropriate consequences to the behavior, commensurate with the level of misbehavior, but remember to compliment and reward good behavior whenever or wherever it occurs, especially the little things.

Be sure consequences are sensitively appropriate and not vindictive. Do not yell or get emotional when applying them but make the consequence somewhat *uncomfortable* for the child, so it will be a deterrent to future bad behavior. As we do with puppies, you can choose different consequences for different children, depending on what each will consider *just uncomfortable enough* to change their minds. You have flexibility here along with moral responsibility. Don't take your child's disrespectful behaviors personally! Instead, take it as just another call to leadership.

Situation: Fighting between Siblings

Your kids are constantly bickering and fighting, teasing and crying. "Be nice to your brother!" you yell. "Apologize to your sister!" It's like a broken record at your house and you're sick of it.

Understand It:

Rivalry between siblings is as old as the biblical story of Cain and Abel where rivalry between these brothers caused one to end the other's life. Rivalry is on our list of hardwired human instincts; there's no way around it so it's going to happen. The question is, how can a parent mitigate the inevitable and either keep it manageable or even use it to their advantage? The solution is surprisingly counterintuitive, especially in Western culture, the home of equality for all.

In my canine consultations, sibling rivalry and fighting between family dogs is a common issue. Owners are distraught because they have tried so hard to treat each dog equally, given each one a bone, letting each one share the couch with Mommy, and swiftly reprimanding the one that snarks at the other. Imagine their shock when I tell them *they* are the reason their dogs are fighting!

There can be lessons here for parenting. Siblings are never "equal." One may be a straight-A student while another is better at music or art and struggles to maintain a C average. Be careful not to hold both to the same standard of accomplishment. If individual differences in ability and talents are not celebrated, you may inadvertently keep your kids in what I call the Purgatory of Equalness. There is no "equal" accepted by their Inner Animal. Being treated as such predictably triggers *Competition* to be different. This instinctive will to establish one's unique position within the family, in turn, can lead to Rivalry and conflict at the instinctive level. Try to avoid holding all children to the same standard of excellence.

Take Action with Bessy's Instinct-Savvy:

Children, like other animals, are striving to find their place in the family pack and clarify their own identity. When it comes to siblings, their DNA may be similar but *they are not the same,* and this is a good thing when it comes to reducing sibling rivalry! Brothers and sisters often have unique and different abilities. The solution for sibling rivalry and fighting at home can be in the knowledge of animal instinct.

We need to address the matter of resources and our instinct to compete over them. Here's what I mean: If the ultimate resource over which children compete is parental approval and pride, parents could make sure they *diversify* what makes them proud. Being proud of scholastic achievement is easy. So is being proud of athletic ability. But what about artistic talent? Creativity? Those tattoos on your daughter that give you such grief could actually be beautiful expressions of art if you change your perspective. They might even be worth a compliment.

Think about this: If you only have one standard of excellence in your household, only one child can occupy the top rung of that standard. The rest could inevitably become rivals. By having more than one standard of excellence in your household, you let each child have his or her own important platform. Brag about your artist. Talk about your poet or musician. Encourage your creative writer to pen their first book. This approach could reduce sibling rivalry in your family and go a long way to build pride and self-confidence in your kids.

Situation: Rebellious Behavior

Your free-spirited teen has always been a "problem." You've been on her for one thing or another her whole life. Now she's gone and had half her face tattooed. It's like she knows exactly what pushes your buttons and chooses that as her behavior-of-the-week, in spite of your oversight and strong parenting. Even though you can see through her devious behavior, you still get upset but you feel too emotionally exhausted to do anything about it because nothing you've tried so far has worked.

Understand It:

As many psychologists *and animal trainers* will tell you, constant correction or criticism can result in rebellious behavior or worse. If a *dog* feels he is always "wrong" with too much heavy-handed control or criticism, he can eventually give up trying or even lash out. Research shows the same sort of predictable rebellion in children under the same weight of constant criticism. "(Too much) criticism and punishment lead to anger and defiance or secretiveness and withdrawal." (Kenneth Harish, PhD, "The Harmfulness of Criticism" March 8, 2012, *Psychology Today*)

Animal trainers have learned to focus more on what their canine students do right in order to turn around behavior and you can, too.

Avoid Ritzi-Rude, Nitpicking and Constant Criticism:

Stop criticizing and calling out every little thing your rebellious child is doing "wrong."

Think about what constant criticism can do to a child's Desire to be Great or Important. It can squash it like a bug. Just as many dog owners forget to recognize and praise the little things their dogs do right, so do some parents, intent on stopping the "bad" behaviors in their children. They fail to see the forest for the trees. They may not notice the glimmers of good or nice behaviors when that sun peeks out from behind their child's clouds of resistance. It's highly unlikely a child would misbehave *every* waking minute of every day or be without some personal virtue. Don't overlook those virtues! I believe we get what we focus on. In a case like this, if we focus solely on the negative, might we risk affirming a child's belief that they truly *are* "bad"? That would be tragic.

Take Action with Instinct-Savvy and Bessy-Down:

First, take a breath and shake off all feelings of frustration or anger toward your rebellious child. Remember, *it's not personal—it's instinct.* In the animals I work with, rebellion often has its roots in constant criticism and constant denial of their need to be appreciated at home. Once we focus on the good things the dog does, the rebellion diminishes.

With a rebellious child, perhaps work on feeding *their* Need to be Great or Important, which may have been inadvertently starved along the way. Put on your positivity specs and start looking for things to *compliment* in your child, even if you have to dig deep or create something. Are they smart? Good at a particular sport or skill? If they are older, is there something they could teach a younger sibling?

Could you put them in charge of training the family dog? This or any other assignment of responsibility will create the possibility for mastery, a very effective way to affirm your child's feelings of importance and respect in the eyes of others.

Developing a new, more positive Attitude about your children and how you parent them could open new worlds of peace for you and success for them. Having better relationships with your kids is another thing you can add to your list, when practicing Gratitude. It's all moving in the right direction, up the Happy Pyramid.

Children Want a Hero

Every parent wants their child to "love" them, but what exactly is a child's love and where does it come from? Many parents worry that their child won't "love" them if they set rules or enforce boundaries. They believe that their child's love depends on their making sure everything is rainbows and lollipops, protecting them from the uncomfortable parts of life.

I have a different take on a child's love. It is not borne of rainbows and lollipops. From my perspective, the expression of a child's love for a parent is more like Hero Worship. Children look up to their hero. They admire them. They believe the hero can protect them and is capable of meeting every challenge.

Earn your child's respect by being strong, consistent, and dependable. Instead of being permissive because you are afraid to displease your child and lose their "love," be their hero instead. Heroes are strong and fearless! I see many loving children expressing respect and trust in these real-life heroes—their parents.

CHAPTER NINE

FIVE RELATIONSHIP SAVERS
FOR YOU AND THE BIG DOG
IN THE BEDROOM

"The truth will set you free—but first it will piss you off."
—Gloria Steinem, influential leader
1970s Women's Movement

I n this provocative and most likely controversial chapter, I propose the Nellie-Up Action Style in most cases as the appropriate approach for getting what you want from a spouse or partner. This approach works because Nature does not recognize "equal" status in any situations involving *personal* relationships. The only two strategic options we have for getting what we want from others without conflict are Bessy-Down or Nellie-Up. As hard as that is to understand, it's even harder to accept when it comes to marriage and love-life relationships.

Using Nellie-Up with Your Spouse or Partner . . . and Why

Unless you and your partner have agreed that one of you will be the undisputed leader of the family and *you* are that person, you do not have the status to support Bessy-Down actions or strategies for control. If you and your partner have decided that you will each have "equal" say in the relationship or if you have never discussed it and simply assume this is the case, realize that your "equal" relationship is only an intellectual concept. In reality, *instinct and animal nature are most likely to prevail.* Since neither of you has legitimate claim to *higher* status than the other, neither one of you can legitimately make rules or insist on your way. That's Bessy-Down behavior and neither of you is Bessy! Nope. The only way to get what you want from another is, from Nature's perspective, *Nellie-Up.*

If truth be told, Nellie could also have been a marriage counselor!

She is an expert at being liked and trusted. A husband or partner that likes you and trusts you and is not constantly challenged by you is probably more likely to go along with your ideas and desires. It's something my mother knew and used in her life with my father for nearly fifty years. Adopting a Nellie-Up relationship style, she got what she wanted and then some, more often than not.

Lessons in Marriage from My Mother

My mother was living proof that a woman can be strong, effective, and influential, regardless of what she chooses to do with her Monday–Friday life. My mother never held a job outside our home. She was, however, one of the strongest and most indomitable women I have ever known and a very smart wife. In many ways, my mother taught me more than anyone about success in marriage by modeling it for me. (Remember our instinct for Imitation?) She had mastered the art of controlling my father, and that was an art form! He was charismatic, charming, handsome, and successful, but he had been raised an only child and was used to getting his way. He was strong-willed. Mom learned, however, that you get nowhere with confrontation in marriage. Instead, patience and clever influence is the name of the game. Like Nellie, her sense of timing was impeccable. She knew when to push and when to back off; when to give and when to take; and how to use sweet influence instead of nagging to get what she wanted.

My mother understood her partner's need to feel important and respected. She would never embarrass my father by correcting or disagreeing with him in public. She saved that conversation for a more private time. In public, she complimented him regularly. On many occasions I went clothes shopping with my mom, and she would always make her selections based on "what Daddy would like." Given the choice between a shapeless, but comfortable, dress or one that showed off her fabulous figure, she would always take home the latter "on approval," of course. "Your father would like me in this," she would say.

I know you must think this was a downtrodden woman of the time, repressed and controlled, sacrificing her needs for those of her husband. Oh, far from it! You didn't know my mother. She was a formidably strong woman and a brilliant strategist! She knew, in her own way, that if she gave my dad what he enjoyed in these less important areas, he would more happily yield to her wishes in more important negotiations. I don't mean to suggest there was an ulterior motive at play here. My mother simply knew that in marriage, respecting and being friends with your partner and giving them what they want whenever it makes sense to do so, goes a long way toward getting what *you* want. She had a beautiful new house on the hill, custom kitchen, new cars, and a wardrobe the envy of other wives. More importantly, she had a happy relationship of love and mutual respect with her husband. She knew the marriage magic of Nellie-Up!

147

Your Nellie-Up Action Plan
with Your Spouse or Partner

- Refuse to argue. Look for ways to keep the conversation pleasant.

- Speak to them like you did when you were dating, when you wanted them to like you.

- Talk to them, not at them.

- Put yourself in their shoes, try to understand their perspective and treat them like you would want to be treated.

- Always look for ways to feed their desire for Respect.

- Don't shoot down their ideas; acknowledge their merit before you voice your own.

- Do not disagree in public; be a predictable ally.

- Don't do things behind your partner's back.

- Earn Trust; don't destroy it.

- Be patient and agreeable.

- Wait for the right time to ask for something.

- Don't insist on or compete for your way.

- Be willing to take "No" for an answer.

- Be a friend.

The Conflict Twins are Nipping at Your Heels

Let's take a look at some of the most commonly reported problems for Western couples today and understand them from our animal instinct and the happiness principles perspectives. Interestingly, we find a common thread through most of the problem scenarios that follow. It's our old friends, the Conflict Twins, "Same" and "Equal"! Do you remember why they are dubbed the Conflict Twins? It's because our Inner Animal does not recognize same or equal when it comes to relationship *status* and will not rest until a differentiation of some sort is established. In Nature, this is done through challenge and conflict.

In Western marriage and relationships, many couples intellectually agree to equal status between partners, but in practice their instincts may be constantly striving for *differentiation*. This is the great conundrum of marriage: *how to maintain a mutually respectful relationship without yielding to the Conflict Twins and our instinct to compete with and challenge one another.*

In my observation of animals, the more important it is to be Top Dog, the more frequently animals fight. Animals with less pride or less sense of self-importance, however, fight less. There is a profound lesson here for couples entering into marriage or a committed relationship: *Living harmoniously together requires a different skill set than living alone.* A natural Bessy-Boss must frequently adapt to Nellie-Nice if harmony and friendship is to be maintained. Self-interest often needs to take a back seat and this is never easy, especially with the Conflict Twins always whispering in our ear, "There's an empty seat behind the wheel. Grab it now!" With this in mind, let's examine some common relationship issues and ways to solve them.

Situation: Lack of Communication; Not Listening

Your husband works hard at his job. When he gets home, he seems to tune you out and the last thing he wants to do is talk, but it's extending into the weekend as well. He buries himself in his laptop checking email or in front of the TV, watching sports or playing online games. When you ask him a question you get no response, or he might shake his head to affirm a request, such as picking up milk on his way home from work. But the next day he comes home without the milk, and you begin to feel ignored and isolated in the relationship.

Understand It:

There can be several underlying reasons behind this common complaint, and often it's difficult to differentiate one reason from another. Sometimes ignoring someone's request or demand is a subtle expression of power. For example, we would never refuse to respond to our boss when they speak to us but might feel less obliged to respond to a frivolous comment from an employee. By not responding to you at home, the Conflict Twins may be driving your husband to act out a slight power advantage, though he may not even know he's doing it. They are shifty little devils, those Twins!

On the other hand, the reason for his behavior could be a matter of overload. When life gets crazy, we all need some "me time." Without some ability to decompress, today's stressful life-demands can be too much. When "me time" morphs into social isolation, however, that's a different matter.

There's also our basic animal tendency to Avoid the Unpleasant and Seek Pleasure instead. The reasons behind your husband's zone-out may be centered there, and not in a desire to spite or disrespect you. Something might be making the television, online games, and emails *more pleasant* than talking with you at that moment. Though you don't intend to, might your spouse feel like every time you talk to them you are giving an "assignment" or pointing out what they should do better? Too much of that can trigger the instinct to Avoid the Unpleasant, but more importantly, rob a man (or woman) of their deep, instinctive need to feel important and respected.

Avoid Bessy-Boss, Ritzi-Rude and Scaredy-Cat:

You're not the boss of your husband, so be careful not to come across like one (even though the Conflict Twins may be cheering you on!). Bessy-like behavior can certainly cause friction and stir the pot in most marital relationships where you have intellectually agreed to equal standing, one to another. Though his lack of listening is frustrating, and you may take it personally, do not react emotionally to your spouse when he does this. That Ritzi-Rude, over-reactive style can only serve to ignite any anger or resentment that might be smoldering under the surface or, even worse, *create* it. That said, if you simply ignore the issue, like a Scaredy-Cat, nothing will ever improve.

Take Action with Nellie-Up:

Here are some things you might try that have the Nellie-Up Seal of Approval:

- Even when we are in a relationship, we all appreciate a little "me time." Just as we might enjoy a personal, She-Shed retreat, think about giving your husband some Man Cave time and don't interrupt him during it. He may not have an actual Man Cave, but you can give him a virtual one by agreeing that for certain blocks of time, neither you nor the kids will bother him. He can watch sports or play games to his heart's content. My husband decompresses by watching golf or YouTube videos on cars or politics. I don't start up a conversation during this time, but I might sit down quietly with him and watch, too. I tell him I just like his company while I laugh at the funny stuff and show interest in the other, respecting this "no conversation zone" unless he initiates one.

- Outside of Man Cave time, begin the conversation with a personal compliment or interest in his day. Then you could start asking for your spouse's attention or communicate any requests you might have for him.

- Make talking with you a pleasant experience, even when you ask for his action or cooperation on household or other matters.

- Use body language to show you're listening. Mirroring, nodding, etc., are compatible with our Flocking, Similarity and Attraction instinct, as well as that of Group Cohesiveness.

- Don't interrupt when he is speaking. Rephrase what you think your spouse has said. This will feed his Desire to be Important and to be taken seriously.

Situation: Money Issues

You have taken on the household task of paying the bills each month. Since you have always been good with numbers and with money, it made sense. You are very conservative with your spending habits, trying extremely hard to avoid emotional purchases and keeping the family finances in good shape. It's why you are so angry every month when the credit card bill arrives and you see that while you've been saving, your husband has been spending like a drunken sailor! Not really, but it's how you feel when you see the bill. You have asked him repeatedly to cool his self-indulgent spending, but he doesn't stop. Your debt keeps growing, and you're afraid that soon *your* credit rating will suffer because of his irresponsibility.

Understand It:

First and foremost, understand that money issues are not about money. They are about power. Money, after all, is one of our critical resources. Control of a critical resource determines one's status standing within the group—in this case a group of two. With your attempts to limit his spending, you are unintentionally limiting his access to a critical resource and the power it represents. Your money issues are more likely a competition for status. In fact, a husband directed by his wife to reduce his spending can actually feel emasculated. Your husband's ability to "spend" money could be his way of exercising power that he feels otherwise denied. Again, this probably isn't about money but about power and those pesky Conflict Twins that insist on some sort of differentiation in the relationship.

Avoid Bessy-Boss, Ritzi-Rude and Scaredy-Cat:

Clearly, scolding or demanding your husband to spend less or be "more responsible" with money might only serve to deepen his need to prove his importance, and spend more. Getting angry at him could make him dig in deeper. If you ignore the problem because you're afraid of the escalating tension, you could be riding the Scaredy-Cat train to the poorhouse.

Take Action with Nellie-Up:

Be friends, not competitors. Don't act like a Top Dog, guarding or hoarding information about finances; that could be seen as a Bessy power play and create even more conflict. Instead, share financial information like a Nellie. Sit down together and tally up all your basic required expenses for the month (rent, food, utilities, insurance, savings, etc.) as well as your total income. Subtract one from the other and ask if each of you can commit to splitting *what's left over* for personal expenses, even if that requires some adjustment of habits.

When the next credit card bill arrives, don't expect miracles right away, but thank your guy for any improvement you see in his spending. If *you* go off course with your half of the personal spending budget agreement, make sure you fess up to this as well. What's good for the gander is good for the goose. Honesty and openness are the basis of Trust, and Trust is the foundation of your happiness together, whether it's money or anything else. Honesty can diffuse feelings of Competition.

Situation: Housework and Chores

Both you and your husband work all day, but it seems all the household chores are left to you. It doesn't seem fair, and the idea that he just assumes these chores are "women's work" ticks you off. Why should he sit on the sofa drinking a beer while you are scrubbing the toilet?

Understand It:

Recall how every human has a deeply set instinct to Avoid the Unpleasant? Don't expect your partner to jump up and volunteer to clean the bathroom or scrub the floor. Household chores are not pleasant experiences for most people. You would avoid them yourself if you didn't hate a dirty house more. Your spouse is probably not being disrespectful or lazy when he leaves the domestic goddess jobs to you. He's just being normal.

Then again, allowing an unequal chore load might be another unintentional power play orchestrated by the Conflict Twins, Same and Equal. Letting you do more of the chores and him less of them could be a quiet statement about status. The Twins won't let him share 50/50. Why, that would be the "same" and they can't have that!

Avoid Bessy-Boss, Ritz-Rude and Scaredy-Cat:

If you and your spouse have agreed that your marriage is one of shared responsibilities, do *not* be his Bessy and start assigning chores. You are not his boss. Yelling or pouting like Ritzi-Rude when he seems lazy or unhelpful will turn him off to you. Letting resentment build up inside by avoiding the matter like a Scaredy-Cat, however, will likely end in a destructive explosion or toxic internalization.

Take Action with Nellie-Nice:

Getting your husband to help more around the house and dodging the Conflict Twins is a clever ballet, not a cage fight. You can't force his head into the sink until he submits to wash the dishes, but you can exercise your power of persuasion.

This power of persuasion starts with a mutually loving and respectful friendship. Since you must not *order* his help, your spouse must *want* to help you, and this is most likely to happen if he likes you. Yes, it really can be that simple. Everything in a healthy marriage, for that matter, begins with trust, respect, and real friendship. Trust, respect, and friendship are the antidote to the Conflict Twins! You have to like each other for harmonious cooperation to happen. Work on this as the foundation for all your "asks."

Start with a small ask, like carrying out the garbage and thank him for doing it. Let him feel appreciated and valued. Maybe ask him to feed the dogs for you when you are running late, and again thank him when he does. Tell him how much you appreciate him and how good a dog-dad he is. He's the best. Little asks at a time, with lots of appreciation is often a winning strategy. You can make chores more pleasant by association, increase his sense of importance, and reduce his reasons to avoid and leave chores to you. Voila!

Watch Out for 50/50

It's important to point out that literal 50/50 in a relationship can be a dangerous expectation. This is because one party's perception of meeting in the middle can often be perceived by the other as falling short.

Perspectives often differ. When they do, disappointment and resentment can follow on both sides. My advice is for each partner to willingly go *more* than halfway in any 50/50 agreement—even housework. That's what friends do.

Situation: Trust and Infidelity Issues

You just found out your husband had an affair with a coworker before leaving his last job. You are devastated, and it has rocked your relationship to its core. Now you wonder where he is when he is late getting home, you are suspicious of his phone calls, and wonder if he's really on that bike ride with a buddy each weekend.

Understand It:

Trust is everything in any and all relationships. It is Step 1 of the Happy Pyramid and underpins its entire structure. When Trust is damaged or destroyed in a marriage, it can bring the entire relationship down. No wonder this has shaken you to the core. Trust *is* the core.

Avoid Bessy-Boss, Ritzi-Rude and Scaredy Cat:

Though you will feel justified in calling on Ritzi-Rude and Bessy-Boss, it's unlikely that any amount of rage, hysteria or demands for change will rebuild Trust or bring a wayward husband willingly back to hearth and home. And sticking your head in the sand like Scaredy-Cat just prolongs the pain.

Take Action with Every Tool You've Got:

I won't sugarcoat this: Trust issues are potentially the most devastating to a marital relationship, especially if they involve infidelity. Trust must be rebuilt if the relationship is to be healthy going forward. If the wandering spouse is committed to change and the partner is willing to forgive,

Trust may be restored, but with effort. Is it an easy fix? Absolutely not. In fact, it is likely to be the biggest challenge faced by a couple in their marriage. Even with a changed spouse and willing partner, rebuilding broken Trust from infidelity will take time, deep love and supreme effort. The good news is that Trust between partners *can* be repaired, and it can be your greatest personal achievement together.

If, on the other hand, a Trust betrayed cannot be restored, one must face a difficult choice: Stay in a bad relationship and make the best of it or leave it altogether. Neither choice will bring you harmony, but sometimes other factors and responsibilities are greater than our own self-interests. Dependent children, family business arrangements, financial complications, or a spouse's sustainable well-being can outweigh the need for our own happiness. In the end, our Ultimate Happy is truly a personal decision—even the decision not to pursue it.

Situation: The Controlling Spouse

You were enamored by his constant attention to you while you were dating. He wanted to be with you every moment of the day. It was flattering and romantic. Now that you are married, however, this need for togetherness seems more like smothering control than storybook love. Your husband doesn't even like you to go out at night with your girlfriends. He controls the checkbook and the credit cards and makes all the household decisions. You're in a virtual prison and your husband is the warden.

Understand It:

I see controlling spouses as struggling with feelings of personal inadequacies exaggerating their Need to be Great or Important. There may also be a lack of Trust toward their partner. In extreme cases it is often both. Although every one of us has a need to feel important and respected on the status ladder, this type of uber-controlling behavior can point to deeper issues that you should never have to deal with alone. It's one thing to understand why a behavior is occurring but quite another to be equipped to safely handle or change it. *Extreme behaviors require not only your understanding of the Happy Pyramid, but professional help as well. Avoid Going It Alone:*

If you are in a relationship with an over-controlling partner, my advice is to reach out for professional guidance. You may well be sitting on a minefield, and only a professional can help you safely navigate it. Don't take chances.

Take Action with Professional Help:

Many women have spouses who they consider "too controlling," always insisting on having everything their way like choosing the furniture styles you buy, picking the movies you watch, deciding on the vacations you take, etc. (Ironically, I find many *wives* in this controlling category!) In these everyday situations, use the Nellie-Nice approach to rebuild Trust and friendship with your partner as a way to reduce your spouse's everyday need to control.

What I have described in the earlier scenario, however, is control on an entirely different level. When controlling behavior becomes oppressive (forbidding time with friends, constant suspicion, etc.), it could be potentially dangerous. A professional should help you sort out whether your spouse's behavior is extreme or just annoying. *Your path forward will depend on that professional determination.* If the controlling behavior is the run-of-the-mill annoying type, you can probably work through it with the right guidance and a little Nellie-Up. In more difficult cases where physical safety is in question, however, a professional can help get you out of that situation.

There is no doubt that having the support and love of a trusted partner and a successful relationship with them is one of the pillars of a happy, satisfied life. Using these strategies and firming up this foundation gives you one more thing to be Grateful for. It makes it easier to have a positive Attitude toward life and frees you to find that Purpose that will lead you to your Ultimate Happy.

CHAPTER TEN

ULTIMATE HAPPY AND YOUR POWER OF CHOICE

Activating The Seven Steps to Happy and climbing the Pyramid simply requires us to awaken and consciously *choose* the right path and footholds along the way. These footholds vary by situation, by your place in the hierarchy, and by your willingness to choose the tools I suggest. The Happy Pyramid is your grand guide. Copy it. Put it on your refrigerator, on your desk, in your wallet. It is a reminder to keep your focus, to "choose" your best path and use the powerful tools provided to succeed in any situation life might throw at you as you make your way to your Ultimate Happy.

The beauty (and perhaps the difficulty) of the Pyramid lies in the choices required at each Step. Climbing the Pyramid requires that we consciously override our Inner Animal in many instances, especially when it comes to choosing an Action Style in Step #5 that might not come naturally to us. Fortunately, unlike animals that are slaves to their own personalities and instincts, the human animal can and in many cases *must* override their natural instincts and urges in their pursuit of harmony and happiness.

Practicing Happy

Like any other skill in life, Happy takes practice.

I pride myself on being a good cook, but when I first tried my hand at baking bread, I wasn't very good at all. I struggled with getting my dough to rise and where to set the bowl in my chilly farmhouse so the temperature would be just right. Then I needed practice on how to knead the dough, for how long, and how much flour to keep adding. It took many embarrassing attempts and many loaves of dry, tough and nearly inedible product, but I didn't give up or let the fear of embarrassment stop me. I finally got it right, and it's funny how such a little thing made me feel so accomplished. Now I'm not only known as a great cook among my circle of friends, but the Woman Who Even Knows How to Bake Bread. Of course, achieving a happy life is much more challenging than baking bread, but my point is nearly every success is built on tenacious practice and the choice to undertake this practice.

Happy is a goal reached only through choices.

Happy is the result of a series of intentional choices. It doesn't just fall into our lap or happen because we're a good person. That would be like thinking a raging bull won't charge at you because you're a vegetarian! No, achieving a state of Happy takes work, tenacity and conscious, everyday choices.

Overcoming the instincts of your Inner Animal that are blocking your path to Happy takes the same kind of practice as learning any skill. Your defensive Inner Animal and ego might have a knee-jerk, habitual reaction to fire back at certain types of comments made by your spouse, kids or others. Taking a breath and pausing before reacting takes repeated practice, like unlearning any habit. If you are instinctively a go-along-to-get-along type of person, enforcing rules or disciplining your staff or children might be difficult for you; but with courageous practice over time, you can become an effective leader and parent, as well as a beloved one.

Just as a mountain climber hones their skills over many climbs, learning just the right footholds and choosing just the right equipment over time so are able to climb higher and more challenging peaks, so, too, climbing the Happy Pyramid takes similar practice. A serious climber who has their eye on a summit does not give up on their first try if it does not go well. And they don't try to make a huge climb in just one day. They pace themselves and prepare for the long game. If there is a quest, a real desire to conquer the mountain, a climber is in it for the long haul. And their tenacity and attention to detail generally pays off.

Think of our Happy Pyramid as your mountain. Each Step presents different challenges, and each requires certain Choices to be made as a skill set is developed.

Choice: Managing Expectations

One of the fundamentals in any service-oriented business is knowing how to meet a client's expectations. For that reason, successful service businesses are careful to manage expectations from the get-go, being honest and forthright about what they are promising to deliver. Their best outcome is to under-promise and over-deliver.

When it comes to improving a less-than-perfect relationship in our life, or one that is taking up all the oxygen in our room, so to speak, we can train ourselves to analyze the Trust level at Step 1 of our Happy Pyramid. If Trust is an issue with that particular person, we must choose to manage our expectations of relationship bliss. If there is limited Trust—if you do not fully believe in the other person's honesty, integrity, and ability—that particular relationship may not be one upon which you base your climb to your Ultimate Happy. That's not to say you cannot get along with those whose honesty, integrity, and ability you doubt, but they are the "also-rans" in your relationship world, and you must choose to manage your expectations of them. You won't invest too much of your precious emotional capital trying in vain to make the relationship perfect. Spend your greatest efforts on relationships that need work, but the raw materials of Trust are at least in place.

If Trust in *you* is in doubt for the other's perspective, you can choose to get busy rebuilding it, if you can.

Choice: Pushing Ego and Pride Aside

Your Situational Status and Personal Boundaries revealed at Steps 2 and 3 of the Happy Pyramid may not be intuitively obvious and may even seem counterintuitive to you at first. Accepting a Situational Status that is lower than you would like might even offend you. It will take practice and conscious choice to push aside your ego and pride that are blocking your progress.

In the West, and especially the United States, the words in our Constitution, "All men are created equal," has been engrained in us with the assumption that it means we are all the same. In truth, these words reflect the belief that every person born is entitled to equal respect, equal rights and equal opportunity from birth, and not about every human being identical in personality, skills or innate ability. Animals in Nature are all born with the same opportunities to survive and thrive, but it is the individual's talents, efforts and ability to recognize and take advantage of situations in their relationships with others that ultimately determines what they achieve and how well they live. Those animals most successful in life are the ones that do not let pride or ego complicate their Situational Awareness.

Looking at our own social dynamic the prism of our Inner Animal, we can see there's a hierarchy in every relationship, even if subtle. As you analyze relationships based on critical resources and who controls them, you recognize this hierarchy and are ahead of the game. When control of resources is equal or nonexistent and you have no status advantage in the situation (i.e., with friends or coworkers), accepting a Nellie-Nice role rather than Bessy-Boss in that moment becomes easier if Ego and Pride have stepped aside.

In any event, your eventual Happiness will be tied inextricably to your future choices of how you choose to relate to other people, whether it be a Bessy-Boss or Nellie-Nice Action Style. Choose wisely.

Choice: Bravery or Humility

At Step 4, you must accept the role in which your find yourself in the situation. You must either accept to take the role of Bessy-Boss or that of Nellie-Nice. If Bessy-Boss, you must choose Bravery to lead. It takes guts to be a boss. You must do the right thing even if it means not everyone will like you for doing it. It takes Bravery to put yourself out there like that.

If you are called to be Nellie-Nice, Humility will be your path to success. Let's be clear: *Humility is not the same as weakness*. Being humble simply means you realize you don't know everything. You are not perfect. You might know a lot, but someone else will always know more or do it better than you. There is always something to learn (even from your subordinates). Ego and hubris are thin-shelled and destabilizing forces, which can knock you off your Happy Pyramid quicker than you can say, "I'm the Greatest," only to leave you shattered, like Humpty Dumpty. Even from a position of power in a relationship, be you a boss, a parent, etc., choosing humility can be your path to greatness if you take it.

Accepting the best Action Style may be challenging, especially if that status position is more than you think you can live up to, or less than you think you "deserve." And yet, unless you Accept whatever your situational status is at the time and select your Action Style accordingly, your road progressing up the Happy Pyramid will likely be blocked by predictable pushback and conflict, either because you seem too weak, or unjustifiably controlling.

Choice: Distinguishing Your Action Style from Your Personality

Choosing an Action *Style* means you are intentionally choosing to *act* a certain way, not change who you are. The Action Style you are called to follow may not necessarily represent who you are as a person, but that's OK. It's just the game plan you are following to succeed in the relationship at hand. If you are a naturally nice person who needs to assume a Bessy Boss role with subordinates, you can still deliver your rules, expectations and even your consequences in a "nice" way. If you are naturally bossy, learning to act in a Nellie-Nice fashion when required might even improve your leadership skills by softening their edges when they are called upon in other situations. (As an evolved Bessy-Boss myself, you can trust me on this!)

Choice: Positivity

Life is not a child's storybook or a Hollywood romantic comedy, where everything is rainbows and lollypops and the guy always get the girl, or the girl the guy, and wedding bells ensue.

No. Life is full of disappointments, struggles, tragedy and heart-ache—the counterpoints to our joys. successes and happy moments which also occur. Life is a balance, like Nature herself. To everything there's a season, and every situation in life offers an opportunity to view it as either bad or good. The view you choose and how you interpret life and all that happens along its bumpy road is a *choice!*

Choosing Positivity means you realize there are going to be road-blocks, but you believe the detours you're forced to take off your planned routes can reveal glorious new views or experiences. If you instead choose to be sucked into negativity where you fail to see the positive counterpoint in every tough situation, you may miss the detour which can lead to your Happy.

Choice: Gratefulness

Gratitude is at the top of our Happy Pyramid, but it's so easy to feel sorry for ourselves, isn't it? Someone else got the promotion, we've hit a rough patch and are fighting with our husband, we lost someone special . . . it can go on and on. Practicing Gratitude helps keep our perspective and prevents us from falling down the rabbit hole of misery and self-pity. Focusing on our own problems keeps us from helping others with theirs. It weakens our spirit—the spirit necessary for making the Seven Steps and climbing our Happy Pyramid.

Nature calls us to stay balanced and within the life she gives us, there is always a plentitude of things to be grateful for if we choose to acknowledge them. The importance of these unappreciated gifts will far outweigh any temporary troubles. Finding and identifying all that we have to be grateful for—big or small—requires conscious intention, and this is the essence of practicing Gratitude. Choose to be Grateful.

Choice: Finding Your Purpose

We discussed the importance of finding a Purpose at the beginning of the book, but a personal Purpose may not fall into your lap. Or if it does, you may not notice it unless you have *chosen* Purpose as a life goal and have your feelers out. As days and weeks and years fly by, not everyone takes the time to consider their life from thirty thousand feet. The sad irony is that for many people, most of their life has been lived by the time they start wondering, "What's it all been about?" Only then do they begin looking for ways they can contribute something of deeper value to their time here on Earth. One of my friends once said, "I want to do more than just suck up air and take up space." Well said, I think.

Finding Purpose will add a special depth and dimension to your life, but make no mistake: It is a choice. Choosing Purpose is one of the best ways I know to conquer the summit and plant your flag at the top of your Happy Pyramid: *Ultimate Happy.*

CONCLUSION

In sharing Nature's simple secrets of living your best and happiest life, I hope that ***Harvest Your Happy*** has provided you with new insights and hope. My goal is to give you an easy, practical guide to simplifying life, empowering your effectiveness through harmony with others, finding more meaning in life and ultimately becoming truly Happy. I hope it has inspired you!

Now you know your path to that wonderful state is not as complicated as you might have thought. Getting there is as simple as knowing the Seven Secrets and climbing the Seven Steps of the Happy Pyramid, which I designed based on the secrets of Mother Nature and her contented Kingdom. From my no-nonsense Farm Girl perspective, I have taken you on a journey up the Pyramid by first helping you understand the Inner Animal in all of us and the hidden instincts that can be influenced to your advantage without conflict. As you climb each Step and reach your personal goals with less pushback, you are building and cultivating happier relationships which enable you to finally Harvest Your Happy with the addition of some very human elements: Attitude, Gratitude and Purpose. These elements are the final Step of the Pyramid and set you up to grab the proverbial ring and achieve Ultimate Happy.

In my life and in my work, I am a devotee of the beauty and balance of Nature. I detest jargon that makes simple things sound more complicated than they are. There is a purity and harmony in the simple ways of the natural world that needs no embellishment. A fresh look at relationships and at yourself sweeps away confusion and opens a simple path to your success. I am honored to have revealed Nature's wisdom to you.

You now have the secrets to getting Happy in life: Secrets left behind in the pristine obscurity of Nature that I've dusted off and presented with a practical guide you can use every day.

Now, go Harvest Your Happy!

REFERENCES

Introduction

(p xx) Wohlleben, Peter (2017). Greystone Books, Ltd. *The Inner Life of Animals,* n.p.

Part I

Chapter One

(p 4) Maslow, A.H. (1943). *A theory of human motivation* (http:// psychclassics.yorku.ca/Maslow/motivation.htm)

(p 5) "Study on Adult Development" Harvard, (1980-2010)

Chapter Three

(p 27) Harari, Yuval Noah (2015). HarperCollins, *Sapiens*, 18.

(p 28) Angell, James Rowland (1904). *Psychology: An Introductory Study of the Structure and Function of Human Consciousness*—Ch. 16: "The Important Human Instincts."

(p 29) Berscheid, Ellen, and Walster, Elaine H. (1969). *Rewards Others Provide: Similarity in Interpersonal Attraction,* 69–91. Reading, MA: Addison-Wesley.

(p 29) Belz, Michael and Pyritz, Lennart W. and Boos, Margaret (2012). "Spontaneous flocking in human groups," n.p.

(p 38) Dewey, John (1859–1952). American philosopher, psychologist, Georgist and educational reformer. One of the fathers of functional psychology.

(p 38) Freud, Sigmund (1856–1939). Founder of modern psychoanalysis. Introduced the concept of the id, the ego and the super-ego

(p 40) *New York Times*/Carl Sefina. "Think You Know What Alpha Male Means? These Wolves Will Prove You Wrong" (July 5, 2015). Interview with Rick McIntyre, veteran wolf researcher.

Chapter Four

(p 57) Carnegie, Dale (1936). Simon and Schuster. *How to Win Friends and Influence People.*

Chapter Five

(p 64) Cain, Susan (2013) Crown, *Quiet: The Power of Introverts in a World That Can't Stop Talking.*

(p 65) Cialdini, Robert B. (1984). HarperCollins, *Influence: The Psychology of Persuasion.*

Part II

Chapter Seven

(p 82) Entrepreneur.com (Feb 3, 2003). "When Employees Miss Deadlines."

(p 91) *Harvard Business Review*/Nigel Nicholson (July–Aug 1998*).* "How Hard-Wired is Human Behavior?"

(p 95) Crowley, Katherine (2012). McGraw-Hill, *Mean Girls at Work.*

(p 100) *Harvard Business Review*/Tony Schwartz (June 18, 2012). "Share This with Your CEO."

Chapter Eight

(p 141) *Psychology Today*/Kenneth Harish Ph.D, (March 8, 2019.) "The Harmfulness of Criticism"

I hope you enjoyed this book. If so, and you think others would enjoy it too, would you do me a favor?

Like all authors, I rely on online reviews to encourage future sales. Your opinion and recommendation would be invaluable. Might you take a few moments now to share your assessment of my book on Amazon or any other book review website you prefer?

If you enjoyed this book, your positive review and recommendation can help many others lead, succeed and live their best life.

My sincere thanks . . . and may you revel in your Ultimate Happy!

Camilla Gray-Nelson

ACKNOWLEDGMENTS

This book began as an idea that I felt compelled to share. I knew the information could be as precious as a gem, but needed expert shaping, cutting, polishing and setting in order to sparkle and realize its full value. I am so grateful to the handful of talented professionals that helped make this happen. Most importantly, I want to acknowledge my amazing developmental editor, Claudia Riemer-Boutote, Red Raven Studio, who through our many months of friendship, collaboration, creativity, and inspiration helped cut and polish my manuscript so that it could shine most brightly. I also want to thank my friend and informal literary advisor, Terri Leonard, who first encouraged me to push forward and develop my ideas into a book. Finally, a thank you to my talented publicist, Julie Baker, who completed the team by "setting" my little gem in its best light and helped bring it to the public.

ABOUT THE AUTHOR
CAMILLA GRAY-NELSON

Best-selling author and award-winning entrepreneur with a company consistently listed in the Top 15 Women-Owned Businesses in Northern California, Camilla Gray-Nelson has a leg up on her competition. Raised and living on a farm, Camilla credits her business success today to the lessons she learned from Mother Nature in her childhood! Combining a keen knowledge of animal behavior and her awareness of the human animal's inner instincts, she reveals Mother Nature's paradigm to all women who seek their own success at work, parenting and love. She shares the animal secret of *Influence through Instinct* to more cleverly succeed in getting what we want in our professional as well as personal lives, while at the same time, maintaining precious Peace and Harmony . . . two seemingly "endangered species" in today's chaotic world!

YOUR
QUICK GUIDE
TO HAPPY

*Feel free to cut out and use these
pages for daily inspiration*

THE HAPPY PYRAMID

ULTIMATE
HAPPY

7. HAPPY WITH MYSELF
I live with a positive Attitude,
Gratitude and Purpose

6. HAPPY WITH OTHERS
I replace friction with cooperation

5. GETTING ALONG & REACHING GOALS
I activate my *Influence, Instinct, and Action Style*

4. ACCEPTANCE
I accept this present arrangement

3. PERSONAL BOUNDARIES
I realize the limits and expectations of my present position

2. SITUATIONAL AWARENESS
I understand my "pecking order" in this particular situation

1. TRUST
I believe in the other's character, honesty and ability

Seven Steps to Happy: The Pyramid
©2023 Camilla Gray-Nelson

The Seven Secrets

(That animals know and you should, too)

1. Humans are animals, too!

2. Instincts rule . . . intellect plays catch-up

3. We can't all be Top Dogs . . . and that's OK

4. Beware the Conflict Twins: "Same" and "Equal"

5. Know your rung

6. The Negotiation Elevator goes Up or Down . . . never Sideways

7. Choose the right shoes for the conversation

Your "Action" Archetypes

Bessy-Down

- Calm, focused and kind

- Makes rules and expectations clear

- Unafraid to follow through

Nellie-Up

- Fosters friendship and trust

- Requests, does not demand

- No entitlement, and ego in check

Your Bessy-Down Action Strategy

For Relating to Kids, Employees and Staff

- Be the living example of what you expect from them
- Communicate your rules and expectations clearly
- If possible, establish a reward system for goals met
- When rules are broken, do not yell, berate or over-react
- Use Bessy's 3-Step Follow-Through
    a. Give a low-key reminder or warning
    b. Formalize disapproval and clarify expectations for change
    c. Take more serious action if expectations are not met
- Follow through and enforce rules or boundaries without apology
- Stay calm and on message; factual
- Always consequence with explanation
- Always end a disciplinary conversation expressing your belief in them and belief that they can do better going forward
- Be the boss but be nice about it. Be likable

Your Nellie-Up Action Strategy

To Use with Bosses, Spouses, Coworkers and Friends

- Earn their trust and admiration

- Live your loyalty; be a predictable ally

- Foster friendship and harmony

- Don't make demands or give "orders"

- Avoid arguments or conflict

- Wait for the right moment to ask for something

- Frame your requests in a way that demonstrates the benefit to the other person

- Be willing to graciously take "No" for an answer; don't insist or pout

Harness the Power
of Farm Girl Attitude

- Resilience and Humility

- Self-Reliance

- Patience

- Respect for Nature and Reality

- Nurturance

- Courage

- Hope and Optimism

Our Inner Animal Instincts

- Avoiding the Unpleasant or Difficult

- Grouping

- Flocking and Similarity Attraction

- Fear/Distrust of the New or Unfamiliar

- Classification/Profiling

- Hierarchy

- Loss Aversion

- Rivalry

- Jealously and Envy

- Curiosity and Secrecy

- Shyness and Sociability

- Imitation

- Constructiveness

- Sex and Reproduction

- Desire to be Great or Important

My Gratitude List

I am grateful for these things in my life. I will acknowledge them every day and live in a state of Gratitude

-
-
-
-
-
-
-

My Purpose Journal

"Our prime purpose in this life is to help others."
—The 14th Dalai Lama

How might I help others in my community or my world in an ongoing way?

Made in the USA
Monee, IL
24 March 2023

30351792R00129